"This book cuts to the very heart of the core principles of statistical inference and does so in a way that is accessible and easily digestible. I honestly wish a book like this one had existed when I was a student – I would have clutched it hard and never let it go!"
Dr. Ruth Horry, *Senior Lecturer in Psychology, Swansea University, UK*

"I see this book as a very useful resource, not only for those who have just started their journey at the university, but also for senior students to experience "aha!" moments while recapping the basics from a unique and nicely presented perspective. I am looking forward to recommending this book to my students as soon as it is available".
Dr. Krzysztof Cipora, *Lecturer in Mathematical Cognition, Loughborough University, UK*

"As a new graduate student, I was suddenly faced with academic papers presenting statistical methods. But with hardly any statistical understanding myself, I struggled to do this well. I longed for a book that I could easily refer back to. This is that book. The explanations are very accessible, the examples are relatable, and the book is concise. I thoroughly recommend it".
Jennifer Read, *Graduate Student in Education, University of Derby, UK*

"If you want to understand why we use statistics in psychology, this is the book for you!"
Dawn Short, *Ph.D. student in Psychology, Abertay University, UK*

"This is an accessible and helpful educational tool that students with a variety of backgrounds will enjoy. The author incorporates clear examples and is able to frame advanced concepts in a simple and straightforward way".
Dr. Dawn Weatherford, *Associate Professor of Psychology, Texas A&M University, San Antonio, USA*

Psychological Statistics

Psychological Statistics: The Basics walks the reader through the core logic of statistical inference and provides a solid grounding in the techniques necessary to understand modern statistical methods in the psychological and behavioral sciences.

This book is designed to be a readable account of the role of statistics in the psychological sciences. Rather than providing a comprehensive reference for statistical methods, *Psychological Statistics: The Basics* gives the reader an introduction to the core procedures of estimation and model comparison, both of which form the cornerstone of statistical inference in psychology and related fields. Instead of relying on statistical recipes, the book gives the reader the big picture and provides a seamless transition to more advanced methods, including Bayesian model comparison.

Psychological Statistics: The Basics not only serves as an excellent primer for beginners but it is also the perfect refresher for graduate students, early career psychologists, or anyone else interested in seeing the big picture of statistical inference. Concise and conversational, its highly readable tone will engage any reader who wants to learn the basics of psychological statistics.

Thomas J. (Tom) Faulkenberry, Ph.D., is Associate Professor and Head of the Department of Psychological Sciences at Tarleton State University in Stephenville, TX (USA). A mathematician by training, he teaches courses on statistics and mathematical modeling in the behavioral sciences, and his primary research areas are mathematical cognition and Bayesian statistics.

The Basics Series

The Basics is a highly successful series of accessible guidebooks which provide an overview of the fundamental principles of a subject area in a jargon-free and undaunting format.

Intended for students approaching a subject for the first time, the books both introduce the essentials of a subject and provide an ideal springboard for further study. With over 50 titles spanning subjects from artificial intelligence (AI) to women's studies, *The Basics* are an ideal starting point for students seeking to understand a subject area.

Each text comes with recommendations for further study and gradually introduces the complexities and nuances within a subject.

FRENCH REVOLUTION
Darius von Güttner

RESEARCH METHODS (third edition)
Nicholas Walliman

ARCHAEOLOGY (fourth edition)
Brian M. Fagan and Nadia Durrani

REAL ESTATE
Jan Wilcox and Jane Forsyth

MANAGEMENT (second edition)
Morgen Witzel

SEMIOTICS (fourth edition)
Daniel Chandler

For a full list of titles in this series, please visit www.routledge.com/The-Basics/book-series/B

Psychological Statistics

The Basics

Thomas J. Faulkenberry

Routledge
Taylor & Francis Group

NEW YORK AND LONDON

Cover image: © Getty Images

First published 2022
by Routledge
605 Third Avenue, New York, NY 10158

and by Routledge
4 Park Square, Milton Park, Abingdon, Oxon, OX14 4RN

Routledge is an imprint of the Taylor & Francis Group, an informa business

© 2022 Thomas J. Faulkenberry

Library of Congress Cataloging-in-Publication Data
A catalog record for this title has been requested

ISBN: 978-1-032-02096-9 (hbk)
ISBN: 978-1-032-02095-2 (pbk)
ISBN: 978-1-003-18182-8 (ebk)

DOI: 10.4324/9781003181828

Typeset in Garamond
by KnowledgeWorks Global Ltd.

Contents

Preface

My goal in writing this book is to give more people a chance to *really* understand statistics. Whether you are a first-year student or a recently-awarded Ph.D., I hope this book will help you to make better sense of how statistics works, especially in psychology and the behavioral sciences.

Given the size of this book, you might consider this goal as a fool's errand. Surely there is not enough material covered in this book to offer anyone a deep understanding of statistics. Right?

In some ways, you are absolutely correct. A quick glance at the numerous statistics textbooks on the shelf in my office tells me that a deep knowledge of statistics requires careful reading of many pages. One popular introductory textbook that I just randomly pulled off the shelf contains 18 chapters and 770 pages (with very small typeface). Moreover, there are many such books on my shelf. These books have it all (well, almost). As a *reference* book, these books are matched by few.

But few people can just *read* these books. In my experience, that's not how students learn statistics. Why not? Well, for one, the sheer size of these traditional textbooks can be intimidating. Students don't find them approachable. I know this because my students tell me this all the time. Also, these books tend to be very expensive. With the ever-increasing costs of attending universities in the United States (Sherman, 2020), expensive and encyclopedic are not necessarily the things I'm looking for when trying to find a textbook for my students.

Frustrated by this, I asked the following question one day on Twitter:

> "I wonder if there's a demand for a *very short* introductory textbook for statistics in psy/behav-sci. Seriously...like less than 100 pages. I'm so tired of encyclopedic intro texts that have (imo) too much material. Thinking about writing a true 'getting started' text".

The response was quick and clear. I received a number of positive reactions, particularly among my followers who were early career psychologists.

People clearly want to make sense of statistics. One of my followers offered the following:

> "Anyone producing such a book would be the hero of psychology undergrads everywhere! I had 5 stats textbooks and I've graduated with little more understanding of stats than when I started".

This book represents my attempt to deliver what I offered that day. I hope you enjoy it as much as I've enjoyed writing it.

In many ways, this book will be quite unorthodox. As I already mentioned, it is designed to be a very short book. It is also unique in its simple approach. Whereas traditional statistics textbooks are often written in a mathematically rigorous style and offer a comprehensive approach to coverage of topics, this book is decidedly informal and quite limited in its scope. My goal is not to teach you how to carry out a vast array of statistical methods for all kinds of different experimental designs, but rather to give you an overview of the *process* of statistical inference. To this end, I sacrifice rigor and topic coverage in order to give the reader a focused and enjoyable read. My tone is conversational. I want the reading experience to feel like a dialogue, with questions (and their answers) being the driving force to guide the narrative.

Finally, this book is unorthodox in that it does not rely on a specific computer software package. Computers are indispensable tools for doing statistical inference, and for analysis of big, complex data sets, they are the *de facto* way of going about things. But in my almost 25 years of teaching mathematics and statistics, I have repeatedly observed that teaching introductory statistics *via* computer software is very difficult. In most cases, the course becomes a course on how to use the software, not a course on *how statistics works*. There is ample evidence to suggest that the traditional approaches to teaching statistics to our psychology students (e.g., increasingly broad topic coverage, teaching through specific computer software packages, etc.) has not resulted in students understanding the *what* and *why* of statistics, even when they become researchers themselves (Gigerenzer, 2004; Hoekstra et al., 2014).

I don't blame the students, nor do I blame their teachers. I think the problem stems from the growth of statistics as an essential tool for our field. One natural consequence is that our statistics courses become so packed with material and move so quickly that students become overwhelmed, and much like a rock climber, they have to find the smallest thing to hold on to in order to survive the experience. Usually, that thing is the p-value. But instead of learning what a p-value is and how to correctly interpret it, students usually only remember it as a magical divining rod for statistics: if $p < 0.05$, then we have *found something*, and if not, then we didn't. As our field is beginning to realize, the didactic, ritualistic application of p-value thresholds to our science is not moving us any closer to truth. If anything, the focus on making decisions with *p*-values has led to questionable research practices and a corresponding call to rethink its use (e.g., Wagenmakers et al., 2011).

Against this backdrop, my primary aim is to help you learn the *process* of statistical inference. We will focus on learning the concepts, not just how to work a bunch of problems. While I will certainly present example problems and provide exercises for you to work through, the purpose of these problems is to exemplify and reinforce the *concepts* that cut across all statistics. In our work in psychology and the other related behavioral science, we design experiments and observe data. In this book, you'll learn three core tenets which allow us to make sense of these experiments and data: (1) how we describe the observed data; (2) how we can build *models* for the observed data; and (3) how we can compare competing models of the observed data. Additionally, you'll be introduced to Bayesian model comparison, an increasingly popular method of inference which in many ways can be a very useful (and easy to interpret) tool.

To wrap up, I should say a word or two about computer software. I am a big proponent of open source software, and specifically I am an early adopter (and big supporter) of the free software package JASP (JASP Team, 2020). I have even written tutorial papers (e.g., Faulkenberry, Ly, & Wagenmakers, 2020) and a free textbook (Navarro, Foxcroft, & Faulkenberry, 2019) to advocate its use. However, to maintain the focused and software-independent nature of this book, I have decided not to include it as a tool here. When we do need computational power to compute things (e.g., *p*-values and Bayes factors), we will use a free interactive web application called PsyStat, which I developed specifically for this book. I will first describe its use in Chapter 3, but you can go ahead and take a look at it by navigating your web browser to https://tomfaulkenberry.shinyapps.io/psystat. There are a couple of advantages of this app over a computer software package like JASP. First, it is platform independent – it works as well on any computer, regardless of operating system, but it also works on any mobile device. All that is needed is access to the internet. A second advantage is that it requires no installation – all computation is done in the cloud. You'll simply see the results on your device. I hope you like it.

I am grateful to many people who have been instrumental in the development of this book. First, I would like to thank Lucy McClune from Routledge, who responded to my call on Twitter and gave me the confidence to even pursue this work. The entire editorial staff at Routledge has been so helpful throughout this project. I would like to thank the many students who have taken my introductory statistics course, most of whom have gotten to experience firsthand the approach to learning statistics that I am sharing in this book. Specifically, I appreciate the many helpful and spirited conversations with Kristen Bowman, Keelyn Brennan, and Bryanna Scheuler. I would also like to thank Amber Bozer, Krzysztof Cipora, Ruth Horry, Jennifer Read, Dawn Short, and Dawn Weatherford for reviewing an earlier version of this book. The variety of perspectives and expertise they brought in their comments has strengthened it greatly. I would also like to thank all my colleagues at Tarleton State University for their support and encouragement throughout the writing of this book. And finally, I would like to give special thanks to my wife Eileen and my children Emily, Elena, and Will. I am fortunate to have a spouse in academia and three very smart children who appreciate and understand two parents who get paid to "think about stuff".

I hope you enjoy this book, and I hope it helps you get closer to *really* understanding statistics.

Chapter 1

A (very) brief introduction to statistical inference

Many books on psychological statistics begin with a discussion about *why* statistics is important. Like those books, we will also begin with such a discussion.

But this is one of the only ways in which this book is like the other statistics books. I'll say more about this later.

So, why will you – the reader – benefit from learning statistics? Why is statistics important in the field of psychology?

I am often presented with this question, especially at informal gatherings. It is usually difficult for me to answer the question succinctly. Since I teach statistics and do research to develop new statistical methods, I perceive so much beauty in the theory and practice of statistics that I want the listener to perceive it in an equally vivid fashion. Ultimately, the limitation of time intervenes and I am left resorting to some wholly unremarkable answer such as "Well, in psychology we are often interested in treatments and interventions, and we use statistics to find out if they worked".

This answer usually makes me cringe as soon as it leaves my lips. Yes, it is true, but it is very shallow. There is so much more to psychological statistics. Look at the size of any contemporary textbook for statistics in the behavioral sciences. They're huge. In fact, these textbooks are often so big that they become difficult to read. What they achieve in comprehension becomes a barrier to the beginner who wants a concise introduction to the subject. That is exactly my aim in writing this book.

Let's talk about the *basics* of psychological statistics.

I am a behavioral scientist, so most of the descriptions I will give throughout the book will be born from the context of doing research. But everything I will describe is equally applicable to psychologists as practitioners too; I'm just not as familiar with that world. As a researcher, I study numerical cognition, so I am interested in understanding how people think about numbers. This is a big aim, so let's scale it back a bit. One very specific phenomenon that interests me is something called the *size congruity effect* (Henik & Tzelgov, 1982), which I can easily describe. In laboratory experiments, researchers in numerical cognition often ask people to quickly choose the larger among pairs of numbers presented

DOI: 10.4324/9781003181828-1

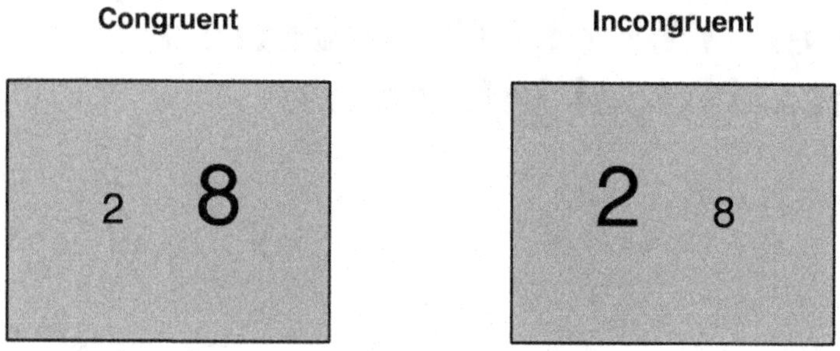

Congruent   Incongruent

Figure 1.1 Two types of trials in a number size comparison task.

on a computer screen. For example, we might ask people to choose the number with the larger *physical* size – two examples are presented in Figure 1.1.

It probably seems like an easy task, right? All you need to do is look for the physically larger number and indicate it with a button press – for example, press the left arrow key if the larger is the number on the left, and press the right arrow key if the larger is the number on the right. Indeed, it is an easy task, as people usually complete each of these comparison trials in less than a second. But there is something subtle about how we perceive numbers lying just below the surface. Let's dig deeper.

In these experiments, we purposely present people with two different types of trials. In one condition (see the screen labeled "Congruent" in Figure 1.1), the physically larger number is also the numerically larger number. We call these trials congruent because the relationship implied by physical magnitudes is aligned with that implied by the numerical magnitudes. But in the other condition, you'll notice that the physically larger number is the numerically *smaller* number. These trials are called "incongruent". Perhaps surprisingly, people are ever so slightly slower on these incongruent trials (usually about 50–60 milliseconds). That is, even though the task only requires us to pay attention to the physical size of the numbers, the numerical magnitude of the numbers seems to interfere with this decision. Surely we could just ignore the numerical magnitude and focus our attention solely on the physical size of the digits?

It turns out that the answer is "no". People are slower on the incongruent trials; that is, they exhibit a "size congruity effect". But how can I justify this claim?

Well, that is the point of this book. We will use the tools of **statistical inference** to provide justification of this claim. To motivate your reading of the rest of the book, let's walk through a "30,000-foot view" of the process of statistical inference.

When I ask a specific question about human behavior (e.g., are people slower on incongruent trials?), I am ultimately engaging in a very hard exercise. I am trying to answer something about a lot of people (ultimately, the entire human **population**), but I cannot possibly test every single person. Thus, I must resort to testing a relatively small subset, or **sample**, of this population and then using those data to infer something about the larger population.

To do this, I set up an experiment and collect data in order to test competing **models** of that specified human behavior. Here, I use the term "model" to refer to any quantitative instantiation of some behavior. These statistical models are a bit different from the types of models you may have previously encountered during your study of the psychological sciences, such as the multistore (i.e., modal) model of memory of Atkinson and Shiffrin (1968) or the Big Five model of personality (Goldberg, 1993). Whereas these models are used to qualitatively understand the structure of some psychological construct (e.g., memory and personality, respectively), a statistical model is purely a quantitative abstraction. In a sense, a model is our best guess about what is going on at the population level.

For example, let us define the size congruity effect as the difference in average response times between the two types of trials – that is, the average response time for the incongruent trials minus the average response time for the congruent trials. Now, let us consider two potential models for this behavior:

- Model 1: the size congruity effect is equal to 0, and
- Model 2: the size congruity effect is greater than 0.

Let's discuss what these models mean. Model 1 says that the size congruity effect is equal to 0, which means that there is no difference between the average response times for congruent and incongruent trials. On the other hand, Model 2 says that the size congruity effect is greater than 0, which means that the average response time for incongruent trials is larger than the average response time for congruent trials. Clearly, these two models make very different predictions about human behavior. Model 1 says that, on average, congruent trials and incongruent trials take the same amount of time to complete. If Model 1 holds, then it would imply that numerical magnitude and physical magnitude are separate things, and that there is no interference between them. On the other hand, Model 2 says that, on average, incongruent trials are slower than congruent trials. If Model 2 holds, then it would imply that numerical magnitude interferes with the physical size judgment, which would mean that the two different types of magnitude are inextricably linked.

So which model is the "right" one?

You'll likely notice that at no point in this discussion have we talked about any actually observed data. Instead, we have proposed these two models *a priori*; that is, before observing any data. The models are theoretical. This is how science works – we propose competing explanations (models) and then verify these explanations against observed data. We have our models, so let's collect some data – and this is where statistical inference comes in. Once we have the observed data, we engage in **model comparison**, which amounts to a single question: which model best predicts our observed data?

Almost everything we do with statistics in the psychological and behavioral sciences comes down to three things: describing data, setting up models, and figuring out which of those models best explains the data we've observed. This is illustrated nicely in Figure 1.2.

Figure 1.2 is an example of the Kanizsa (1976) triangle illusion, and it serves as an excellent framework for understanding how psychological statistics works. The three components I just mentioned serve as the three anchors of the figure. Importantly, if you look at the figure just right, you may perceive a triangle that pops out of the middle between the three Pac-Man-shaped anchors. It is important to note that the triangle is not physically there – rather, it is an inferred object that we perceive. This "illusory triangle" serves as a strong metaphor for our scientific quest of things that are impossible to see. From the three concrete anchors of describing our data, defining models, and comparing the models, we are able to see the answers we seek in our pursuit of knowledge of how the mind works.

From this vantage point, I can offer a simple answer to the question of "why statistics?": it is the tool that allows us to see the unseeable in our scientific pursuits.

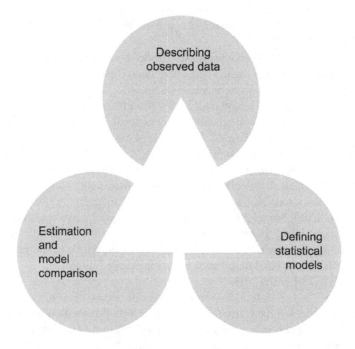

Figure 1.2 A framework for psychological statistics based on the Kanizsa (1976) triangle illusion.

Chapter previews

To conclude this short introductory chapter, I will walk you through how we will engage these anchors so that scientific truth will "pop out". But before that, I want to convince you that even though my example is very specific to numerical cognition and seems to live solely in the world of theoretical research, the idea of model comparison is central to all aspects of the psychological sciences. As I mentioned earlier, practitioners of psychology might be interested in understanding how to test whether some treatment works. After all, if the treatment doesn't work, why administer it? In this context, we can do something similar to what we did above. For example, before administering the treatment, we can set up two *a priori* models: one where the treatment works (i.e., people who undergo the treatment score higher – or lower – on some outcome than people in a control group), and one where the treatment does not work (i.e., no difference in outcomes between the treatment group and the control group). Then, after observing some data, we can compare the models against these observed data. If the first model predicts the data better than the second model, then we have evidence that the treatment works. If the reverse holds, then we have evidence against the efficacy of the treatment. Either way, we learn something very important about this treatment.

Now, let's walk through the process of statistical inference and foreshadow the content of the upcoming chapters.

The first thing we'll do is *describe our data*, which we will cover in detail in Chapter 2. This allows us to communicate to others the most typical measurements in our study. In Chapter 2, we will specifically cover two of the most common summary measures: the *mean* and *median*. But describing the most typical measurement is not enough; we must also communicate how much these measurements vary among the individuals in our study. To do this, we will learn the concepts of *variance* and *standard deviation*, which index on average how much each data point differs from the mean. Combining the concepts of center (i.e., mean) and variability (i.e., standard deviation) gives us a very powerful tool to use in model comparison, which is the ability to *standardize* a dataset into something called z-scores. As it turns out, z-scores will be essential for assessing how well our observed data are predicted by the various theoretical models that we can develop.

After learning how to describe and standardize observed data in Chapter 2, we will learn how to construct potential models of the observed data. This will require two chapters. In Chapter 3, we will focus on the *normal distribution*, which is a simple model of many observed behaviors in psychology and the behavioral sciences. Distributions allow us to think about data using the tools of *probability*. For example, if we suppose that the size congruity effect is 0 (i.e., Model 1), we can use the normal distribution to compute the probability of a single person having a size congruity effect of 50 milliseconds or larger. If this probability (called the p-value) is very small, this might begin to tell us that Model 1 is unlikely to have produced our observed data (leading us to reject this model in favor of the other model, Model 2). Sound easy? It is...and computing these probabilities is easy too, especially with a simple web-based application called *PsyStat*, which I will introduce in Chapter 3.

After getting accustomed to computing probabilities of single observations from normal distributions in Chapter 3, we will extend our discussion to how to compute such probabilities for *multiple observations* in Chapter 4. Specifically, I will describe how to construct the *distribution of sample means*. This will be an important distribution for us – because we use the mean to describe our multiple observations, our questions will be about the likelihood of getting our specific sample mean under a specific model. It turns out that this distribution of sample means is also normal, so that means everything we learn in Chapter 3 will be applicable here.

Now the moment we've been anticipating is here – how do we compare the two models of our observed data? Chapter 5 will give us a way to do it. Specifically, I will introduce the classical techniques of *estimation* and *hypothesis testing*. In estimation, we will use the tools of Chapter 4 to work backward from our observed sample mean and compute an interval which we can use to estimate the unknown population mean of our theoretical distribution. Then I will introduce hypothesis testing, which involves defining two competing models like the ones above. This works by assuming that Model 1 (also called the *null hypothesis*) is true and computing the likelihood of observing our sample mean (or more extreme) under that model. This probability (the p-value) is then totally natural to compute using the methods of Chapter 4. If this p-value is small, it tells us that Model 1 does not predict our data well, which in turn tells us (in an indirect way) that Model 2 is the better model.

In Chapter 6, we will encounter the critical role of *assumptions* in our statistical models. Here, I will point out that the previous chapters have all demonstrated situations where the population's standard deviation is assumed to be a known value. Thus, this chapter is driven by asking what happens when we are not given the population standard deviation. This gives the opportunity to discuss how to estimate the (unknown) population standard deviation from our observed *sample* (what some books call the "sample standard deviation"). After describing this, we encounter the problem that our distribution of sample means no longer follows a normal distribution, but rather something entirely different. This new model (the t-distribution) is then described (along with a bit of its interesting history), and I describe how to perform estimation and hypothesis testing with this t-distribution. Fortunately, the concepts do not change – just the underlying model – so the t-test is then presented as a simple extension of what we already know how to do from Chapter 5 – that is, defining competing models, observing data, then computing the likelihood of the observed data under Model 1.

Whereas Chapter 6 concludes our discussion of the classical techniques in statistical inference, Chapter 7 will present a more modern approach. In this chapter, I revisit the classical model comparison methods covered in the earlier chapters and describe two fundamental limitations of using the p-value as an index of model adequacy. First, I will point out that p-values only assess the fit of Model 1 (the null model), and as such, the support for Model 2 is only indirect. Second, I will point out that p-values never lend us support for the null – only against. Given this, I will introduce an alternative pathway to model comparison – *Bayesian hypothesis testing*. Specifically, I will introduce the *Bayes factor*, which is the relative likelihood of the observed data under both Model 1 and Model 2. In addition to calculating Bayes factors, we will discuss how to interpret them and calculate the *posterior probability* of the winning model, something that p-values do not give us.

Finally, in Chapter 8, I will take us back through the statistical journey that we've traveled, hopefully helping to demystify the concept of statistical inference. Then, I will briefly discuss the next steps that you might want to take, including a conceptual discussion of additional hypothesis tests that you may perform in your future research endeavors (e.g., two-sample t-tests, analysis of variance, correlation, and linear regression). I also briefly describe some software resources that you can use for more complicated datasets, including the free software packages JASP (https://jasp-stats.org) and jamovi (https://www.jamovi.org).

At this point, if things don't quite seem to make sense, that's OK! After you read through the book, I invite you to come back to this chapter and read it again. I bet you'll find that more things make sense. In fact, the book is short, so you can read it *multiple times*, and each round should shine a bit more light on your understanding of these fundamental concepts.

This is a short book, but it contains some deep ideas. Be careful – after reading, you might actually want to learn more about statistics! I hope so, anyway. Let's get started.

Supplementary video lecture

If you would like to watch an online video lecture where I discuss the concepts we talked about in this chapter, you can navigate your web browser to https://youtu.be/KT-VNOa_bfI. Really, you only need to watch the first 8 minutes, as the remainder of the video picks up with material related to the next chapter.

Chapter 2

Describing the observed data

There are many ways to describe data. Indeed, most comprehensive statistics textbooks take three or four chapters to cover all the ways of describing data, ranging from numerical summaries to graphical depictions. This is all important stuff, and it often forms the core of some introductory courses on statistics. But our goal in this book is model comparison, not data description. Thus, I don't want to spend too much time on it. Instead, we will focus our discussion to the key properties that are usually considered when describing data:

- describing the **center** of a dataset, and
- describing the **variability** of a dataset.

I'll specify exactly what I mean by "center" and "variability" in the next two sections. But first, let me assure you that my choice to focus on center and variability is not arbitrary. You may recall from my foreshadowing in Chapter 1 that most of this book will focus on using things like the **normal distribution** to serve as theoretical models of the kinds of data we observe in psychological and behavioral contexts. One of the reasons that the normal distribution is a popular model is that it is very easy to describe – in fact, it can be completely specified by two numbers (or **parameters**), both of which represent the same kinds of things we are about to talk about. Specifically, those parameters are μ (pronounced "mew"), which represents the center of the distribution, and σ (pronounced "sigma"), which represents the variability (or width) of the distribution. So, the things we're about to spend time on in this chapter are critical, not only for the simple act of describing data but also for a deeper understanding of the more theoretical things we'll be concerned with in later chapters.

Describing the center of a dataset

Data rarely consists of a single observation. Instead, we usually are faced with many observations – a set of data, or dataset, if you will. So how can we take a dataset with many observations and describe it simply? The most common way to do this is to describe the *center* of the dataset; that is, one number that

DOI: 10.4324/9781003181828-2

somehow best represents all of the measurements in the dataset. You have probably encountered this idea before, and indeed may already be familiar with the three primary measures of center: *mean, median,* and *mode.* Let's consider each of these separately.

The mean

The **mean** of a dataset (also known as the *average*) is one of the most frequently used measures of center. Computing the average is conceptually easy – one simply adds all of the measurements and divides the resulting sum by the number of measurements. We can use mathematical notation to express this idea concisely:

$$\bar{X} = \frac{\sum X_i}{N}.$$

Before working through an example together, let's take a closer look at the symbols used in this formula, as we will see things like this frequently through-out the book. The symbol $\bar{X}$ (read as "X bar") represents the mean of our data-set. The symbol $\sum$ is a common way to indicate that we are taking a "sum" (or adding a bunch of things together). The things we are adding together are the individual measurements X_1, X_2, etc., which we compactly denote as X_i. What is that little i in the subscript? That is an "index" variable – it is a way to abstractly represent all of the different measurements $(X_1, X_2, \ldots X_N)$ in one symbol. Finally, the N represents the number of measurements in our dataset.

Let's do a quick example. Suppose we want to find the mean of the following dataset:

2, 3, 5, 8, 12.

As we just saw, to compute the mean, we take the sum of the measurements in the dataset and divide by the number of measurements in the dataset. There are five measurements here, so $N = 5$. Applying our formula for mean, we have:

$$\begin{aligned}
\bar{X} &= \frac{\sum X_i}{N} \\
&= \frac{2+3+5+8+12}{5} \\
&= \frac{30}{5} \\
&= 6.
\end{aligned}$$

So what does a mean of 6 tell us about this dataset? One thing it tells us is that 6 is a *typical* measurement for this dataset. That might seem a bit strange, though, as the number 6 does not appear in the original dataset. In this sense, the mean 6 is serving as a (very simple) *model* for the dataset. Imagine you were trying to describe this dataset to someone else. Would you rather say "I obtained 5 measurements, and they were 2, 3, 5, 8, and 12", or would you rather say "I obtained 5 measurements that were, on average, equal to 6". I know there is not a lot of difference in the difficulty of writing (or saying) those two sentences, but imagine the stark difference that would appear if we had a dataset with $N = 100$ measurements. The value of communicating a simple description with a single number should quickly become apparent in such a case.

Before describing the other two common measures of center, let us quickly think more deeply about this notion of taking the mean 6 as a model for the dataset. A natural question would be, "How well does this *single* number 6 represent this *more complex* set of 5 measurements?" What we are really asking is, "How well does the model *fit* the observed data?" You may remember from Chapter 1 that this is one of our fundamental questions in statistical inference, and we're already asking it, even in this simple case of computing a mean. One way to measure model fit might be to consider how much, on average, each of the measurements differs from 6. If the number is small, that would mean that the fit is pretty good (i.e., the measurements are not too different from 6). On the other hand, if the number is large, that would mean that the fit is not as good, as the measurements would be quite different from 6. We will revisit this idea soon when we talk about describing the *variability* of a dataset.

Median and mode

Throughout this book, we will almost exclusively use the mean as our pre-ferred measure of center. However, there are two other measures which deserve mention – the *median* and the *mode*. Again, as you are probably familiar with these already, I'll just briefly describe them, and more importantly, I'll discuss where they might be better measures to use.

The **median** of a dataset is, quite literally, the *middle* of the dataset. Critically, this assumes that the measurements are numerically *ordered* (either increasing or decreasing). For example, consider the dataset we just used for computing the mean: 2, 3, 5, 8, 12. In this case, the measurements are already in increasing numerical order, so the median is the middle number 5. Like the mean, this number represents a "typical" measurement in the dataset. But, it is different from the mean, and that is a good thing in some cases (more about this below).

In the previous example, there were an odd number of measurements. In such cases, the median will always be one number in the middle, and that number is, by definition, the median. What happens when there are an *even* number of measurements? To answer this, let's modify our example slightly and compute the median of the following dataset:

2, 3, 5, 8, 12, 400.

In this case, having an even number ($N = 6$) of measurements means that we no longer have a single number in the middle, but rather a *pair* of numbers, 5 and 8. When this happens, we define the median to be the average of these two numbers – that is, $(5 + 8) / 2 = 6.5$.

This example illustrates another fundamental property of the median. Notice that I constructed this example by simply tacking on an additional (rather extreme) measurement of 400. This measurement would be considered an *outlier* – that is, it has an extreme value compared to the rest of the dataset. However, even in the presence of this outlier, the median didn't change much (it only moved from 5 to 6.5). It still represents a typical value that we would expect to obtain in this dataset. In this sense, the median is *robust* or *resistant* to outliers. What about the mean? Let's compute it:

$$\bar{X} = \frac{2 + 3 + 5 + 8 + 12 + 400}{6}$$
$$= \frac{430}{6}$$
$$= 71.67.$$

Whereas tacking on an extreme measurement of 400 only changed the median from 5 to 6.5, the mean changes from an original value of 6 to a new value of 71.67! Clearly, the mean no longer represents a typical value to be expected in this dataset. As such, the mean is highly influenced by outliers. It is easy to see why – when computing the mean, the value of the outlier is figured directly into the sum, but for the median, the actual value of the outlier is ignored. So, in situations where one might have the possibility of outliers (i.e., *skewed* datasets), the median is usually a better number to report as the center. Some examples of this include home prices, salaries, and even response times in behavioral experiments (see Miller, 1988).

Finally, let's consider how to report the center of a dataset where measurements are not on a typical numerical scale of measurement. For example, suppose we conducted a survey and recorded the school classification for each of 100 respondents, collecting the following:

- 25 Freshman students;
- 32 Sophomore students;
- 14 Junior students;
- 29 Senior students.

What is the center of this dataset? Said differently, what is the most "typical" classification? We certainly cannot compute the mean, as it makes no sense to add these classifications (what is "Freshman + Sophomore"?). Similarly, we cannot compute median, because such classification-type measurements do not typically admit a natural ordering to them (one could argue that Freshman is less than Sophomore, etc., but surely that depends on context). So, what is left? In this case, we would compute the **mode**, which is the most *frequently* occurring measurement. Thus, our mode would be "Sophomore", the most frequently reported classification.

As you can see, median and mode are important measures to know and certainly have their advantages with certain types of data. However, for the remainder of this book, we are going to focus our attention on the mean. There are lots of other books and papers written on doing statistical inference based on medians and modes (e.g., Wilcox, 2010; 2017), but that is not for us to consider here. After all, our goal is to focus on "The Basics!", so let's not get sidetracked.

Describing the variability of a dataset

When describing the center of a dataset, we are primarily concerned with giving a single value which represents a typical measurement in our dataset. Describing variability is a different goal. Instead of describing the typical measurements we can expect in our dataset, variability is concerned with how the individual measurements differ from this typical value. Often, different authors will refer to variability using terms such as **spread** and **dispersion**. These are good terms to help develop an intuitive feeling for the qualities of a dataset that variability describes. Indeed, datasets with a small amount of variability do not have much spread or dispersion around the center, whereas datasets with a large amount of variability are "more spread out" or "more dispersed".

So how do we measure the variability of a dataset? We will focus on one method here, though keep in mind that there are a lot of other ways we could do this. The method I'm about to describe just happens to be a good one for many reasons that matter later on. As I just mentioned, variability is concerned with how the individual measurements in a dataset differ from the typical measurement. Let's focus our attention on one specific definition of "typical" and consider the *mean*. Then, to measure variability, we simply could ask the following question:

"How much, on average, does each number differ from the mean?"

This should be an easy question to answer. Let's walk through how we might attack this problem. Recall that our example dataset contained the measurements 2, 3, 5, 8, and 12. Also recall that we computed the mean of this dataset to be $\overline{X} = 6$. So, how much, on average, does each of these numbers differ from 6?

The problem with doing mathematics in a purely verbal, intuitive fashion is that you and I might answer this problem differently. For example, how much does $X_1 = 2$ differ from the mean $\overline{X} = 6$? Is it $6 - 2 = 4$, or is it $2 - 6 = -4$? Both answers make sense in some way of thinking. So, we need to be very specific (and consistent) in how we approach problems like this. To promote a systematic way of thinking about this problem, let's do the following: let's compute a **deviation score** for each measurement X_i. A deviation score is simply the difference between the measurement X_i and the mean $\overline{X}$. As a mathematical expression, we would write this as $X_i - \overline{X}$. Since we have multiple deviation scores to compute (one for each measurement in our dataset), it will be helpful to collect these into a table:

X_i	$X_i - \overline{X}$
2	−4
3	−3
5	−1
8	+2
12	+6

Now let's compute the mean of the deviation scores – this will tell us, on average, how much each of our measurements differs from the mean $\overline{X} = 6$:

$$\text{Mean deviation} = \frac{-4 + -3 + -1 + 2 + 6}{5}$$
$$= \frac{0}{5}$$
$$= 0.$$

We immediately have a problem. Our intuitive approach to measuring variability – namely, finding the average of the deviation scores – results in a value of 0 for variability. But this doesn't make sense! Surely, if variability is to be a meaningful descriptor, this dataset should have *some* amount of variability – not 0. So, what is going on here?

Clearly, the issue lies with the deviation scores, and particularly the fact that the sum of the deviation scores is 0. In fact, this is a mathematical property of *all* deviation scores. You can prove that for any dataset, the sum of the deviation scores $X_i - \overline{X}$ is equal to 0. Thus, definining variability as the "average deviation score" turns out to be fairly useless. We need to do something different.

Upon further inspection, you might suspect that the problem stems from the fact that some of the deviation scores are negative, whereas others are positive. If we could somehow get rid of the negatives, our notion of "average deviation score" would no longer suffer from the fate it did above. Indeed, this could work two ways. We could take the absolute value of each deviation score, which we would write as $\left| X_i - \bar{X} \right|$. Alternatively, we could *square* each of the deviation scores, which we would write as $\left(X_i - \bar{X} \right)^2$. Both methods will cause all deviation scores to become positive, so which do we choose?

Certainly either way could work, but for reasons that go way beyond the scope of this book, we are going to choose the second option – let's *square* all of the deviation scores and find the average of those (see Wilcox, 2010, for some discussion of why one might instead choose to use absolute deviations). To do this, we simply need to extend our table from above and make a new column for the squared deviations:

X_i	$X_i - \bar{X}$	$\left(X_i - \bar{X} \right)^2$
2	−4	16
3	−3	9
5	−1	1
8	+2	4
12	+6	36

Now, let's find the mean of those squared deviations:

$$\text{Mean squared deviation} = \frac{16+9+1+4+36}{5}$$

$$= \frac{66}{5}$$

$$= 13.2.$$

Thus, we find that the mean squared deviation is 13.2. This number describes the average of the *squared* deviations of each measurement from the mean $\bar{X} = 6$. Further, this number gets a special name; it is called the **variance** of the dataset, and as a formula, the variance can be written as:

$$\text{Variance} = \frac{\sum \left(X_i - \bar{X} \right)^2}{N}.$$

Don't be intimidated by the fancy formula – it is just a compact way of writing exactly what we just did, which we can summarize in a simple list of actions:

1 we computed the mean $\bar{X}$ for the set of measurements;
2 we computed the deviation scores for each measurement X_i;
3 we squared each of the deviation scores;
4 we added all the squared deviations and divided by N.

There you have it – the variance is simply the average squared deviation. The problem is that as a descriptor of variability, the variance has a problem. Specifically, it is too big! Remember, we began our discussion by proposing to measure variability as the average amount that each of our measurements X_i differs from the mean. We computed a variance of 13.2 – does this mean that, on average, each of our measurements differs from the mean $\bar{X} = 6$ by 13.2 points?

Well, no.

Remember, to compute the variance, we had to *square* each of the deviation scores to get rid of the negatives. Thus, the variance is not the average deviation, but rather the average *squared* deviation. The problem with this is that we don't typically think in terms of squared deviations. As such, the variance is simply on the wrong scale! But there's an easy fix – if we want to go from "squared deviations" to regular deviations, all we need to do is take a square root. Let's do that! Using a simple calculator, we can compute the square root of the variance to be $\sqrt{13.2} = 3.63$. Now, while this number is not exactly the same thing as the "average deviation" (remember, that's always equal to 0), this number is on the same scale as our measurements, so we can roughly interpret it as "On average, our measurements differ from the mean by 3.63 points".

To me, this is a much more useful measure of variability. Like variance, it also has a special name – it is called the **standard deviation**. This name conveys the intuition that we want (an "average" deviation), but since average deviations are always 0, we avoid naming our measure of variability something that is mathematically inconsistent.

As a formula, standard deviation can be expressed compactly as:

$$\text{Standard deviation} = \sqrt{\frac{\sum\left(X_i - \bar{X}\right)^2}{N}}.$$

Again, this formula may look intimidating, but remember that it just expresses what we've already done. That is, standard deviation is the square root of variance. Remember,

• Variance is the average of the *squared* deviations from the mean, and
• standard deviation is the square root of the variance.

Before moving on, let's work through another example. Let's compute the mean and standard deviation of the following set of exam grades from nine students:

96, 84, 72, 84, 84, 93, 96, 87, 78.

First, we'll compute the mean, which we recall is simply the sum of the measurements divided by the number of measurements in the dataset ($N = 9$):

$$\bar{X} = \frac{\sum X_i}{N}$$
$$= \frac{96 + 84 + 72 + 84 + 84 + 93 + 96 + 87 + 78}{9}$$
$$= \frac{774}{9}$$
$$= 86.$$

As the mean represents a typical measurement in our dataset, we can expect the grades among these nine students to be reasonably close to $\bar{X} = 86$. How close? That depends on the variability – to that end, we'll now compute the standard deviation. But first, we must compute the variance, which is the average of the squared deviations from the mean. As I described above, I like to do this in a table, as it keeps everything tidy and easy to follow. First, let's compute the deviations from the mean $\bar{X} = 86$ for each of the measurements X_i:

X_i	$X_i - \bar{X}$
96	+10
84	−2
72	−14
84	−2
84	−2
93	+7
96	+10
87	+1
78	−8

Since we know that the deviation scores $X_i - \bar{X}$ must always add to 0, this will be a good check to perform on such calculations. Indeed, we can verify that:

$$10 + (-2) + (-14) + (-2) + (-2) + 7 + 10 + 1 + (-8) = 0,$$

so we have some reasonable assurance that we computed the deviation scores correctly. Now, let's square each of these deviations so that we can get rid of the negative signs:

X_i	$X_i - \bar{X}$	$\left(X_i - \bar{X} \right)^2$
96	+10	100
84	−2	4
72	−14	196
84	−2	4
84	−2	4
93	+7	49
96	+10	100
87	+1	1
78	−8	64

To compute the variance, we simply find the average of those squared deviations:

$$\text{Variance} = \frac{100 + 4 + 196 + 4 + 4 + 49 + 100 + 1 + 64}{9}$$

$$= \frac{522}{9}$$

$$= 58.$$

Remember, this is the averaged *squared* deviation. To put things back on the same scale as the original measurements, we need to take the square root of the variance, giving us the standard deviation:

$$\text{Standard deviation} = \sqrt{58}$$

$$= 7.62.$$

Thus, this set of exam grades has mean 86 and standard deviation 7.62. This means roughly that, on average, each of the grades differs from the mean $\bar{X} = 86$ by 7.62 points.

Using center and variability to standardize datasets

At this point, you know the basics of describing the center and the variability of a set of measurements with the mean and standard deviation. However, there is another application of the mean and standard deviation that will prove to be useful throughout the rest of this book. To motivate this application, consider the following scenario.

Suppose you are on a committee to consider applicants for an academic scholarship. Both applicants are from the United States and have submitted scores on one of two standardized college entrance exams that are commonly used there – the Scholastic Aptitude Test (SAT) and the American College Test (ACT) (see Croft & Beard, 2021, for a history of these tests). Suppose we see that Applicant 1 scored a 1270 on the SAT, whereas Applicant 2 scored a 30 on the ACT. Which applicant has the most competitive score?

Without more information, this is a difficult problem. Certainly, we cannot directly compare the two scores, as they are on two different measurement scales. We need a way to get them onto the same scale. One way would be to convert the ACT score to an SAT score. Another way would be to do the reverse (convert the SAT score to an ACT score). A third alternative (the one we will pursue) involves converting them both to a standardized score that we'll call z-scores.

Here is how we use z-scores – instead of working with the raw scores for each test, we instead re-scale the scores by asking "how many standard deviations is each applicant above/below the mean?" To figure this out, let's first consider some background descriptive statistics about the tests themselves. For the SAT, the nationwide mean is 1060, with a standard deviation of 210. For the ACT, the mean is 21 with a standard deviation of 6. So, we can quickly see that both applicants are *above* the mean on their respective tests. The question that remains is "how far above the mean?" We can use the standard deviation as a "yardstick" for this.

Applicant 1 scored a 1270 on the SAT. This is $1270 - 1060 = 210$ points above the mean. Since the standard deviation is also equal to 210 points, this is equivalent to saying Applicant 1 scored *1 standard deviation above the mean*. On the other hand, Applicant 2 scored a 30 on the ACT. This is $30 - 21 = 9$ points above the mean. Since the standard deviation for ACT scores is 6 points, 9 points is equivalent to $9 / 6 = 1.5$ standard deviations. So, we can say that Applicant 2 scored *1.5 standard deviations above the mean*.

By computing the distance from the mean in terms of standard deviations, we can easily see that Applicant 2 has the more competitive score. If we step back and take a look at what we've done, it is actually quite clever. We've taken two *completely different* tests and used their respective means and standard deviations to put them both on the *same scale*. This standardized scale is called a *z-score*. Mathematically, z-scores are computed by first finding the difference between the raw score and the mean, and then dividing this difference by the standard deviation. In symbols, this looks like the following:

$$z = \frac{\text{Raw score} - \text{mean}}{\text{Standard deviation}}.$$

To make this more clear, let's consider another example. In my lab, people usually complete trials on a basic mental arithmetic task with a mean of 1200 milliseconds and a standard deviation of 300 milliseconds. Let's compute and interpret a z-score for a trial completed in 800 milliseconds.

First, we compute the z-score:

$$z = \frac{\text{Raw score} - \text{mean}}{\text{Standard deviation}}$$

$$= \frac{800 - 1200}{300}$$

$$= \frac{-400}{300}$$

$$= -1.33.$$

The obtained z-score of $z = -1.33$ means that this trial is 1.33 standard deviations *below* the mean. Notice also that the z-score is a *unitless* quantity. That is, in the numerator, the units are milliseconds, and in the denominator, the units are also milliseconds. When dividing these two numbers, the units divide out, leaving a number with no units. This is a good thing for this application, as it literally allows us to compare measurements on any one scale to measurements on another (possibly different) scale. Of course, this is true statistically – you need some subject domain knowledge to know whether such a comparison makes sense.

To conclude our discussion of z-scores, let's go back to our original dataset that we used to motivate our computations of mean and standard deviation. Recall that the mean and standard deviation of this set of measurements was 6 and 3.63, respectively. Using these, let's convert each of the measurements to z-scores by subtracting the mean and dividing by the standard deviation:

X_i	z_i
2	$(2-6)/3.63 = -1.10$
3	$(3-6)/3.63 = -0.83$
5	$(5-6)/3.63 = -0.27$
8	$(8-6)/3.63 = 0.55$
12	$(12-6)/3.63 = 1.65$

Now, let's compute descriptive statistics for this collection of z-scores. First, we compute the mean (which we'll denote $\bar{z}$):

$$\bar{z} = \frac{-1.10 + (-0.83) + (-0.27) + 0.55 + 1.65}{5}$$

$$= \frac{0}{5}$$

$$= 0.$$

Interestingly, it turns out that the mean of the z-scores is 0. What about the standard deviation of the z-scores? Let's compute the squared deviations:

z_i	$z_i - \bar{z}$	$\left(z_i - \bar{z}\right)^2$
−1.10	−1.10	1.21
−0.82	−0.82	0.68
−0.27	−0.27	0.08
0.55	0.55	0.30
1.65	1.65	2.73

From here, we can compute the variance of the z-scores as

$$\text{Variance} = \frac{1.21 + 0.68 + 0.08 + 0.30 + 2.73}{5}$$

$$= \frac{5}{5}$$

$$= 1.$$

Taking a square root, we immediately get a standard deviation of $\sqrt{1} = 1$. So remarkably, the mean and standard deviation of the collection of z-scores is 0 and 1, respectively.

I'll repeat this for emphasis, while simultaneously adding the assurance of a bigger mathematical fact – when we standardize a collection of scores into z-scores, the mean of the z-scores is *always* 0, and the standard deviation of the z-scores is *always* 1. It may be hard to see why this is important now, but let me assure you, this is a *really* nice property to have. We'll use it a lot very soon.

Chapter summary

Let's recap what we learned in this chapter:

1 At its simplest, describing a set of measurements boils down to describing the *center* of the dataset and the *variability* of the dataset.
2 There are three commonly used measures of center: *mean*, *median*, and *mode*.
3 The mean (or average) is found by adding the values of the measurements in a dataset and dividing by the number of measurements.
4 The median is the middle number when the set of measurements is put in numerical order. If there are an even number of measurements, the median is the average of the two middle numbers. Medians are resistant to outliers (i.e., extreme measurements), whereas means are not.
5 The mode is the most frequently occurring value among a set of measurements. The mode is good to use for data which are not measured on a numerical scale.

6 There are two main ways to describe variability: *variance* and *standard deviation*.
7 The variance of a set of measurements is the average of the squared deviations between each of the measurements and the mean.
8 The standard deviation is the square root of the variance. We usually use
   standard deviation instead of variance when describing data because standard deviation is on the same scale as the original measurements.
9 Mean and standard deviation can be used to *standardize* scores into z-scores,
   which express each measurement in terms of its distance from the mean
   divided by the standard deviation.
10 When a set of scores is transformed into z-scores, the mean of the z-scores
   is 0 and the standard deviation of the z-scores is 1.

Supplementary video lecture

If you would like to watch an online video lecture where I discuss the concepts
we talked about in this chapter, I have recorded two such videos for your enjoy-
ment. For the first video, you can navigate your web browser to https://youtu.be/
KT-VNOa_bfI. If this link looks familiar, it is because you already may have
watched the first part of this video at the end of Chapter 1. Discussion about
center and variability starts around the 8-minute mark in the video. The second
video (covering z-scores) can be found at https://youtu.be/Kc6d-0xBDbM.

Exercises

1 Calculate the mean, median, variance, and standard deviation for the following set of scores:

$$3, 10, 7, 15, 5.$$

2 Using the scores in problem 1 above, add 2 points to each score and compute the mean and standard deviation again. What do you notice? In general, how does adding a constant to each score influence the center and
   variability of a set of measurements?
3 For a set of scores with a mean of 85 and a standard deviation of 8, compute the z-score for each of the following raw scores:

$$X = 95, X = 81, X = 101.$$

4 A set of observations with a mean of 74 and a standard deviation of 12 is
   transformed into a *standardized distribution* with a mean of 50 and standard
   deviation of 5. Find the new, standardized score for each of the following
   values from the original set of observations: $X = 59$, $X = 83$. (*Hint: transform
   the original scores to z-scores, then use the z-score formula again with the new mean
   and standard deviation to find the corresponding values of X for each value of z.*)

Chapter 3

Modeling the observed data

In Chapter 2, we introduced the idea of *describing* observed data using the mean and standard deviation. These **descriptive statistics** give us numerical values that help us communicate a dataset's center and variability, respectively. Also, we introduced the idea of z-scores, which allow us to standardize any dataset in terms of each measurement's distance from the mean. This results in a transformed dataset which (by construction) will always have a mean of 0 and a standard deviation of 1.

In this chapter, we will consider a new goal. Instead of simply describing a set of observed data, we will begin to make guesses about where the data came from. In other words, we will begin to **model** the observed data so that we can make inferences.

You have undoubtedly come across the word "model" in other contexts before. When I was a child, I enjoyed putting together plastic models of automobiles. These models captured many of the observable characteristics of the automobiles they were intended to represent. However, they were certainly not *exact* replicas. For example, instead of faithfully reproducing every gear, spark plug, and gasket contained within a real automobile engine, the model's engine was usually a hollow piece of plastic. It looked like an engine from the outside, but none of the detail within the engine was included. Additionally, most of the models I put together did not have moveable steering mechanisms. These were models intended to capture the *appearance* of the automobile – not the mechanical functioning.

Does this lack of detail hinder the usefulness of the model? Absolutely not! In fact, I would argue that this lack of detail was a feature, not a bug. By glossing over many of the minute details inherent in automobile design, the model gave me a simplified view of how automobiles work. The major components were all present, and the relative dimensions of the constituent parts were faithfully reproduced. By getting rid of the details, I could focus on the big picture and learn a lot the about automobiles that I observed in the real world.

Models in the psychological and behavioral sciences are similar to this. When we place a model on something, we are making simplifying assumptions about the measurements that we have observed (or could potentially observe

DOI: 10.4324/9781003181828-3

later). The types of models we use will reflect different goals, depending on the context in which they are used. In this book, we will focus on models of the measurements we observe. However, mathematical psychologists are often interested in models of the underlying processes that *produce* the measurements we observe – these *process models* are very interesting and can be quite complex!

So what exactly *is* a model? A cursory glance at the literature reveals many different uses of the term "model" in psychology. Some researchers build complex models which can be used to understand the mechanisms responsible for some observed behavior. One example is Ratcliff's (1978) drift diffusion model, a very sophisticated mathematical model which explains (with great accuracy) much of the variability in response times for two-choice decision tasks. However, these *cognitive process models* (e.g., Busemeyer & Diederich, 2010; Farrell & Lewandowsky, 2018; Lee & Wagenmakers, 2013) are well beyond the scope of this book.

Instead, we will use models in a much more limited sense. For our purposes, we will almost always interpret the word "model" within the mathematical context of a **probability distribution**. Formally, understanding the mathematics of probability distributions requires quite a lot of background, including calculus. But it is entirely OK to think about probability distributions informally. I like to think of a probability distribution as a *graph* (i.e., a mathematical function) which expresses the likelihood of obtaining all the possible measurements that make sense in a given context. Technically, the values of this graph must be positive, and the area under the curve made by the graph must be equal to 1.

To make our discussion a bit more concrete, let's consider an example. Figure 3.1 represents two models (i.e., probability distributions) that I have placed on the population of all possible ACT scores. Recall from Chapter 2 that ACT scores have a mean of 21 and a standard deviation of 6. Thus, both of my models should also exhibit these characteristics, so the graphs I've drawn in Figure 3.1 both have means of 21 and standard deviations of 6.

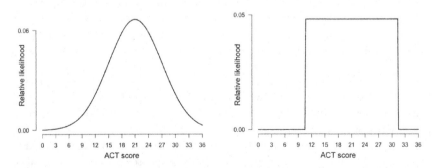

Figure 3.1 Two different probability distributions, or models, with mean 21 and standard deviation 6.

Before getting into the specific differences between these two models, let's consider how they are similar. First, as I just mentioned, both models have a mean of 21 and a standard deviation of 6. This fact is not obvious, and defining the notions of mean and standard deviation for a mathematical function is beyond the scope of this book. But you can *see* the means reasonably well. Notice that the peak of the leftmost graph is directly over the ACT score of 21. Similarly, the flat "box" on the rightmost graph is centered over 21. So, in this sense, both graphs represent what we would expect about ACT scores (at least on average). Soon, you'll learn how to *see* the standard deviation for a distribution as well.

However, the two models are clearly *different* in their appearances. Whereas the leftmost graph in Figure 3.1 is peaked over 21 and the height of the graph decreases as you move to the right and left of 21, the rightmost graph is absolutely flat between the values of 10.6 and 31.4, but it has a height of 0 outside this range. So, which is the better *model* of ACT scores? They both have the same mean and standard deviation, so our search for advantages must go beyond these simple descriptives. I would argue that the leftmost graph is a better model, because the shape of the graph exhibits what I would *expect* about ACT scores. Namely, I would expect most scores to be around 20–22, and scores above and below this range should be less likely to occur. The decreasing height of the graph as you move away from 21 is reflecting exactly this behavior. On the other hand, the rightmost graph does *not* reflect this behavior; instead, it says that every score between 10.6 and 31.4 is *equally likely* to occur. Also, it says the probability of obtaining any score less than 10.6 or greater than 31.4 is 0 (i.e., it cannot occur). The predictions made by this model do not at all reflect what really happens with standardized test scores – certainly, people are much less likely to score a 30 than a 21, and people do indeed score above 31.4 (or below 10.6). For these reasons (and others which we will see very soon!), the model on the left of Figure 3.1 is a much better model.

So why would we want to place a model on our data? Like the plastic automobile models that I made as a child, these *statistical* models allow us "see" our data better, giving us the ability to answer questions that would be impossible to answer using only the observed data. For example, they allow us to assess the likelihood of obtaining our observed data under certain conditions. While that may seem like a strange thing to want to know, it turns out that this question can be very useful to us when trying to assess whether treatments have an effect, or whether there are differences between two groups, etc. Placing models on our data is exactly how we will perform statistical inference – that is, using observed data to infer things about large populations which we cannot possibly measure in an exhaustive manner.

If models are important (and they are), then the next logical step would be to learn which models we should use. This might seem like an impossible task – how can we possibly know which model to place on our data? Shouldn't it depend on the situation? Are models for testing contexts (like the SAT and

ACT) different from those we might use when measuring response times on a behavioral task? Are these altogether different from the types of models I might use when measuring blood-oxygen levels in fMRI scanning studies? It might seem like we've opened a "pandora's box" of possibilities for putting models on data. Indeed, the sky is certainly the limit – there are a lot of models that I *could* place on data. But it turns out that one particular model is extremely useful for the kinds of questions that we often ask in the psychological and behavioral sciences: the **Gaussian**, or **normal distribution**.

The normal distribution

It turns out that you have already seen the normal distribution in this book – it was the leftmost model in my ACT example above. The normal distribution has a classic appearance, with its symmetric, bell-shaped curve. Mathematically, it is a distribution with two **parameters**. That means the normal distribution can be completely described by two numbers: the mean, denoted by the Greek letter μ (pronounced "mew"), and the standard deviation, denoted by the Greek letter σ (pronounced "sigma"). Like all probability distributions, it has a mathematical formula (called its **probability density function**):

$$f(x) = \frac{1}{\sigma\sqrt{2\pi}} e^{-\frac{1}{2}\left(\frac{x-\mu}{\sigma}\right)^2},$$

which when plotted gives the graph in Figure 3.2.

Notice that the graph in Figure 3.2 is peaked at the mean μ and has horizontal symmetry around this value – that is, its shape to the left of the dashed

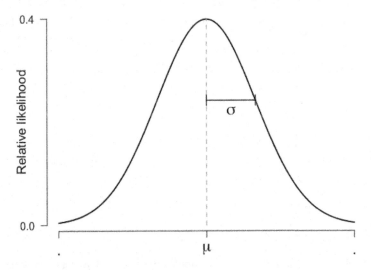

Figure 3.2 Plot of a normal distribution with mean μ and standard deviation σ.

line at μ is exactly the same as its shape to the right of μ. Also, you can see that the width of the curve is determined by the standard deviation σ. Specifically, σ is the distance between the mean and the **inflection point** of the curve. This inflection point is the point at which the concavity of the curve changes from being concave down to concave up.

When modeling our data with a normal distribution with mean μ and standard deviation σ, we can infer many things about these data, because the things that are mathematically true about the normal distribution can be mapped onto statements that are conceptually true for the data. For example, let's consider a few statements that are true about all normal distributions:

- The most likely value of the normal distribution is the mean μ.
- The area under the curve to the left of μ is exactly 0.50. That is, half of the normal distribution is less than mean μ, and half is greater than μ.
- The area under the curve between $\mu - \sigma$ and $\mu + \sigma$ is approximately 0.68 (see left panel of Figure 3.3). This means that we expect 68% of observations to be within one standard deviation of the mean. This further implies that 32% of observations would be outside this range; that is, more than one standard deviation away from the mean. Because the curve is symmetric, this 32% can be divided evenly among the two "tails" of the distribution – 16% would be more than one standard deviation *above* the mean, and 16% would be more than one standard deviation *below* the mean.
- The area under the curve between $\mu - 2\sigma$ and $\mu + 2\sigma$ is approximately 0.95 (see right panel of Figure 3.3). This mean that we expect 95% of observations to be within two standard deviations of the mean. This further implies that 5% of observations would be more than two standard deviations away from the mean, and by symmetry, we can conclude that 2.5% would be more than two standard deviations above the mean, whereas 2.5% would be more than two standard deviations below the mean.

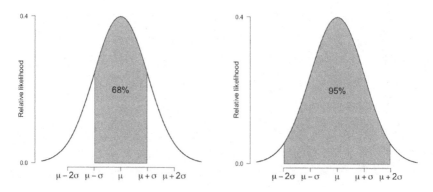

Figure 3.3 Proportions of normal distribution within one and two standard deviations from the mean, respectively.

To make these ideas more concrete, let's suppose we choose to model ACT scores with a normal distribution with mean $\mu = 21$ and standard deviation $\sigma = 6$. Then, we can use the properties above to immediately predict the following:

- The most likely score on the ACT is 21.
- 68% of observed ACT scores should be within one standard deviation (i.e., 6 points) of the mean 21. That is, 68% of test takers should score between $21 - 6 = 15$ and $21 + 6 = 27$.
- 16% of observed ACT scores should be above 27.
- 16% of observed ACT scores should be below 15.
- 95% of observed ACT scores should be within two standard deviations of the mean 21. That is, 68% of test takers should score between $21 - 2(6) = 9$ and $21 + 2(6) = 33$.
- 2.5% of observed ACT scores should be above 33.
- 2.5% of observed ACT scores should be below 9.

Hopefully, the benefit of placing a model on ACT scores is clear. By assuming a particular structure for the population of ACT scores, we get a lot of predictive utility. The model allows us to make inferences about things we have not directly observed. For example, consider my daughter, who at the time I am writing this is about to begin high school. Even though she has not yet taken the ACT, I can reasonably expect her to score between 15 and 27. In fact, I can assign a very specific probability to this statement – that is, there is a 68% chance that she will score between 15 and 27. I also know that there is a small probability that she will score above 33 – namely, a 2.5% chance.

Computing probabilities with the normal distribution

In the examples above, we were able to make specific statements about the proportion of the normal distribution that lies between certain thresholds (e.g., within one standard deviation from the mean, within two standard deviations, etc.). What if we are interested in calculations that do not involve one of these thresholds? For example, we might be interested in knowing the proportion of ACT scores that are below 30. Since 30 is between 1 and 2 standard deviations from the mean 21, we cannot use the properties above to answer this question. So how do we proceed with figuring out what proportion of the curve is below 30?

Before describing how to proceed, I'll briefly mention three ways which we *could* use to approach problems like this. First, problems like this can always be solved using techniques from calculus. Technically, asking for the proportion of scores that are less than a given score is equivalent to asking, "What is the area under the normal distribution curve, up to the value of that specific score?" If you've had a calculus course before, you probably recognize that this is a question that can be answered using *integration*. Of course, if you've never taken calculus, there are other tools available to us that we can solve this problem (though, they do all involve calculus "under the hood").

One of these tools is a classic approach that is still used in many statistics textbooks: the *statistical table*. These tables are usually included as appendices, and they allow us to compute proportions under the normal curve to a surprising level of accuracy. A downside to using tables for these problems is that it is often inconvenient to carry a big statistics textbook around (though in the past, I always made a compact, one-page table for my students to print out and keep with them for the semester). Increasingly, statistical tables are being replaced by dedicated statistics computer software packages. Some freely downloadable packages that are great to use include R (https://www.r-project.org) and JASP (https://jasp-stats.org). Unfortunately, there are some drawbacks to using software (especially for the beginner). For example, both packages require the user to install software on a fully fledged computer; as such, they do not work well (or at all!) on mobile devices such as phones, tablets, or Chromebooks. Later on, when you're doing more sophisticated statistical analyses, these packages will be essential. But for a first pass journey through the world of statistics, they just do too much.

Instead, I am going to demonstrate how to solve problems with the normal distribution using an interactive web application called *PsyStat*. I recently built PsyStat to accompany this book, though it will do a lot more than I will demonstrate here. You can access the app on any internet-capable device (even a very small mobile phone). Just open a web browser and navigate to https://tomfaulkenberry.shinyapps.io/psystat.

When you open the app, you'll be greeted with a user interface that looks similar to Figure 3.4. As of the writing of this book, the app contains two modules: one called *Probability calculator*, and another called *Bayes factor calculator*. The probability calculator is the one that is selected by default, and it is the one we will use now.

Let's walk through a few examples to demonstrate how to compute probabilities with the PsyStat app. First, let's consider the original question we asked: what proportion of ACT scores are *below* 30? To answer this, we will perform the following steps – we'll discuss them in detail shortly:

1 Under "Distribution", choose "Normal".
2 Under "Mean", enter 21.
3 Under "Standard deviation", enter 6.
4 Under "Find Area:", choose "Lower Tail".
5 Under "a", enter 30.

Once you perform these steps, you should see an output similar to Figure 3.4. Specifically, the output gives us two pieces of information. First, it shades the portion of the distribution that corresponds to the choices we made under the "Find Area:" and "a". Second, it gives us the proportion of the curve represented

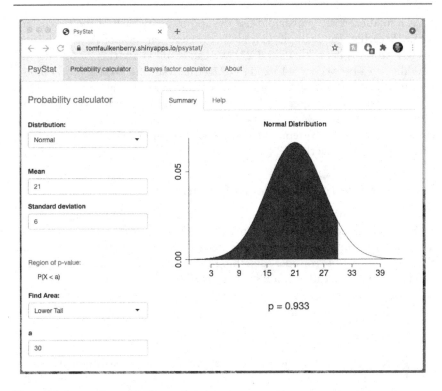

Figure 3.4 Screenshot of *PsyStat* app.

by that shaded area, which in this case is $p = 0.933$. This is called a *p-value* – you can think of it simply as a *proportion* or a *probability*, because that is exactly what it is. For this problem, we can interpret $p = 0.933$ in two equivalent ways.

- 93.3% of ACT scores are below 30, or
- the probability of scoring below 30 on the ACT is 0.933.

Let's continue with another example – what proportion of ACT scores are between 20 and 25? As before, we'll select "Normal" for the distribution, and we'll enter a mean and standard deviation of 21 and 6, respectively. But this time, since we want the proportion *between* 20 and 25, we need to select "Middle" under the "Find Area:" menu. When you do this, the app automatically updates the user interface to ask for *two* endpoints: a (the left endpoint) and b (the right endpoint). For this problem, we'll enter 20 and 25 for a and b, respectively. The resulting output is $p = 0.314$, which like above we can interpret in two ways:

- 31.4% of ACT scores are between 20 and 25, or
- the probability of scoring between 20 and 25 is 0.314.

As a final exercise, you should use the app to verify each of the statements we made earlier. For example, is it really the case that 68% of the distribution of ACT scores is between 15 and 27? We can easily verify this by finding the "Middle" area between $a = 15$ and $b = 27$ – the resulting p-value of $p = 0.683$ confirms that we were right! Similarly, we can verify that approximately 5% of the distribution is greater than two standard deviations away from the mean. To verify this, we select "Both tails" from the "Find Area:" menu and enter $a = 9$ and $b = 33$ (remember where these came from?). You should get $p = 0.0455$ – not exactly 5%, but it's pretty close.

Using z-scores to compute probabilities

You might have noticed that when you first opened the PsyStat app, the fields for mean and standard deviation were automatically set to 0 and 1, respectively. That might seem strange at first – why did I choose to design the app like that? To answer this, consider something that we learned back in Chapter 2 – namely, z-scores. Recall that a z-score is defined as

$$z = \frac{\text{Raw score} - \text{mean}}{\text{Standard deviation}},$$

which we interpret as a way to transform a "raw" measurement into a standardized score that represents that measurement's distance from the mean, using standard deviation as a unit of distance. So, a z-score of +1 means that the measurement is one standard deviation above the mean, whereas a z-score of −1 means that the measurement is one standard deviation *below* the mean. Also recall that if you transform *all* measurements into z-scores, the mean of this set of z-scores is 0, and the standard deviation is 1.

Let's apply this idea to the normal distribution that we've been using to model our data in this chapter. Just like we did with the measurements in Chapter 2, we can transform an entire distribution into z-scores. Mathematically, this looks like the following:

$$z = \frac{X - \mu}{\sigma}.$$

Though it looks different from our definition of z-score in Chapter 2, it says exactly the same thing, just with symbols. X represents our raw scores or measurements; μ represents the mean of the normal distribution; and σ represents the standard deviation. The result of applying this mathematical transformation to the entire normal distribution is called the **standard normal distribution**, and it is exactly what is plotted by default when you open PsyStat for the first time. The only difference in the plot is that instead of having values on the horizontal axis which represent ACT scores, we have values which represent z-scores. Thus, we notice the following:

- The curve is peaked at 0 (i.e., the mean).
- 68% of the curve is between z-scores of −1 and 1 (i.e., one standard deviation below and above the mean, respectively).
- 95% of the curve is between z-scores of −2 and 2 (i.e., two standard deviations below and above the mean, respectively).

So why do I mention this, beyond pure mathematical curiosity? It turns out that the *standard* normal distribution is incredibly useful. Regardless of the scale of my original observed data, if I convert the data into z-scores, I can use the standard normal distribution to model it (assuming that a normal distribution makes sense for the data, of course). That is, I no longer have to specify the values of μ and σ in the app – using the standard normal distribution as a model means that $\mu = 0$ and $\sigma = 1$ by default.

Let's use the standard normal distribution to work through an example. To demonstrate how it works for any context, I'll introduce a new example. IQ scores, such as those from the Wechsler Adult Intelligence Scale (WAIS-IV; Wechsler, 2008) are constructed to be normally distributed with a mean of $\mu = 100$ and a standard deviation of $\sigma = 15$. What proportion of the population has IQ above 110?

To answer this question, let's open the PsyStat app, but this time do *not* change the mean and standard deviation. Instead, let's keep the default values of 0 and 1 for the mean and standard deviation, respectively. Doing this means we are using the standard normal distribution, which requires us to convert the raw score of 110 in our problem to a z-score. For this, we calculate:

$$
\begin{aligned}
z &= \frac{X - \mu}{\sigma} \\
&= \frac{110 - 100}{15} \\
&= \frac{10}{15} \\
&= 0.67.
\end{aligned}
$$

Thus, we translate our question from one involving a specific context – "What proportion of the population has IQ above 110?" – to one which is more general and context-free: "What proportion of the standard normal distribution is above $z = 0.67$?" To answer this, we simply select "Upper Tail:" from the "Find Area:" menu and specify our z-score of 0.67 as the endpoint "a", giving a *p*-value of 0.251. As before, we can interpret this in two equivalent ways:

- 25.1% of the population has IQ scores above 110.
- the probability of having an IQ score above 110 is 0.251.

To fully appreciate the equivalence of the two approaches to computing probabilities that we have demonstrated, you should verify in the app that both methods (using raw scores and z-scores) produces $p = 0.251$. To use raw scores, just enter 100 for the mean and 15 for the standard deviation, and 110 for the value of the endpoint a. You may notice that the p-value is very slightly different at $p = 0.252$; the reason for this is that when we computed the z-score above, I chose to round the repeating decimal 0.6666... to 0.67. This rounding error results in a difference of 0.001 in the two p-values, which is not anything to worry too much about.

A word about mathematical notation

So far, we have been able to work problems involving the normal distribution using mostly verbal descriptions. Soon, however, it will be convenient for us to have a useful mathematical notation for these kinds of problems. Let's motivate this notation with an example. Consider the IQ measurements we introduced above, which we modeled with a normal distribution with mean $\mu = 100$ and standard deviation $\sigma = 15$. There are four types of problems that we could consider, and here are their associated symbolic notations:

1   $P(X < 110)$ – this notation represents the proportion of IQ scores that are *less* than 110. Equivalently, this also represents the probability of having an IQ score less than 110. In the PsyStat app, this area is called the "Lower Tail", which can be selected under the "Find Area:" menu.
2   $P(X > 110)$ – this notation is similar to the first one, but this time we're interested in IQ scores *greater* than 110. Like before, it can be interpreted as either (a) a proportion, or (b) a probability. In the PsyStat app, this area is called the "Upper Tail".
3   $P(90 < X < 110)$ – this one is a little different. It is called a *compound inequality*, and it represents the proportion of scores that are both *greater than 90* and *less than 110*. Visually, this corresponds to the area under the curve between two endpoints. In the PsyStat app, this area is called the "Middle".
4   $P(X < 90 \text{ or } X > 110)$ – this might look similar to #3, but this time, we're interested in scores that are either *less than 90* or *greater than 110*. Visually, this corresponds to the area contained in the *tails* of the distribution, and in the PsyStat app, this area is called "Both tails".

You might be wondering about X. Technically, X is called a *random variable* and is assumed to be modeled by some probability distribution (i.e., a normal distribution). The only time you might see something different is if we're using z scores – in this case, we might write something like $P(z > 2)$. The use of the z variable would tell you that you are using the *standard* normal distribution.

Most of the time, the notation shouldn't get in the way, and the path forward for your computations will be clear from context.

Looking ahead

We have spent a lot of time in this chapter discussing the normal distribution, and you may be wondering whether we are missing an opportunity to discuss other probability distributions that might be more useful for other contexts. I feel as if I should offer a brief explanation of why I have spent so much time on the normal distribution. In Chapter 4, you'll learn about a truly remarkable fact that should completely explain why I've focused on the normal distribution. It turns out that when we take a sample from a population and compute the mean, like we would do if we were doing an experiment, the distribution of all possible sample means that we *could* obtain is very well approximated by the normal distribution. Even more remarkably, it doesn't matter what the original population looked like – if our samples are big enough, this *sampling distribution* turns out to be approximately normal. Thus, our research questions will translate almost exactly to problems that involve calculations with the normal distribution, just like we did in this chapter!

Chapter summary

So what did we learn in this chapter?

1 To better understand the (unobservable) population where our observed data may have come from, we use *models*.
2 A model is a *probability distribution* which tells us the relative likelihood of obtaining the possible measurements that make sense in the context of our data.
3 One common model that is used in a lot of contexts is the *normal distribution*.
4 The normal distribution is completely described by two *parameters*: the mean μ and the standard deviation σ. The normal distribution is symmetric and peaked at the mean μ, and its width is controlled by the standard deviation σ.
5 For any normal distribution, the proportion of scores within one standard deviation of the mean is approximately 68%. The proportion within two standard deviations is approximately 95%.
6 More generally, specific areas under the normal curve can be calculated using tables or computer software. In this book, we will use an interactive web application called PsyStat (https://tomfaulkenberry.shinyapps.io/psystat).
7 The *standard normal distribution* is a normal distribution of z-scores. It has mean $\mu = 0$ and standard deviation $\sigma = 1$. Problems in any context can be translated to the standard normal distribution simply by converting raw scores into z-scores.

Supplementary video lecture

If you would like to watch an online video lecture where I discuss the concepts we talked about in this chapter, you can navigate your web browser to https://youtu.be/ZL8Jtow7IlI. Note that the video talks about an older version of the PsyStat app, but the functionality is virtually identical.

Exercises

1 For a population modeled as a normal distribution with a mean of $\mu = 70$ and a standard deviation of $\sigma = 20$, find the proportion of the population corresponding to each of the following:

   a   having scores greater than 80
   b   having scores less than 86
   c   having scores between 50 and 90

2 Scores on intelligence tests (e.g., IQ scores) are usually standardized to produce a normal distribution with a mean of $\mu = 100$ and a standard deviation of $\sigma = 15$. Find the proportion of the population in each of the following IQ score categories:

   a   Genius or near genius: IQ greater than 140
   b   Very superior intelligence: IQ between 120 and 140
   c   Average or normal intelligence: IQ between 90 and 109

3 Suppose the distribution of scores on the SAT (a college entrance exam commonly used in the United States) is approximately normal with a mean of $\mu = 500$ and a standard deviation of $\sigma = 100$. For the population of students who have taken the SAT, what proportion have SAT scores less than 450 or greater than 600?

4 Over the past 25 years, the university has measured physical fitness for all incoming Army ROTC cadets. During that time, the average score on an endurance task has been $\mu = 17.3$ minutes with a standard deviation of $\sigma = 6.4$ minutes. Assuming the distribution of these scores is approximately normal, find each of the following probabilities:

   a   What is the probability of randomly selecting a cadet with time greater than 20 minutes?
   b   If the university ROTC requires a minimum time of 9 minutes for cadets to pass the fitness requirements, what proportion of the incoming cadets would be predicted to fail?

Chapter 4

How likely is the observed data?

Let's begin this chapter with a hypothetical experiment. Suppose you are working with 10 high school students to help them prepare for their college entrance exams. You have implemented a semester-long training intervention that is designed to help them score as high as possible on the ACT. At the conclusion of the program, your students all take the ACT, and their mean score is $\bar{X} = 25$. A natural question is "Did the training work?"

Much of the rest of this book will be devoted to learning how to answer this question, so clearly it is not a simple one to answer. But we already have enough background to be able to see what is coming, so I'll try to explain as simply as possible. Back in Chapter 1, we discovered that the basic goal when doing psychological statistics was to perform *model comparison*. What that means is that we will use the observed data to compare two competing models – one model where the training actually worked, and one where it did not work. Here, our observed data is a sample of 10 students who took the training and scored an average of 25 on the ACT. Thus, we can ask "how likely is the observed data?" under each of the two models. If the data is more likely under the "training works" model than under the "training does *not* work" model, then we have support for the claim that our training works.

As you can see, our context-laden research question just distills down to a statistical question: how likely is the observed data under some set of competing models? Thus, our goal in this chapter is to learn how to answer the question: "How likely is the observed data?"

In Chapter 3, we already began to see some indications of how to answer this question. There, we learned about one specific model (the normal distribution) that we could place on our observed data. But there is an important issue that we should consider here before beginning to apply this work to answer our question above. First, note that earlier we used the normal distribution as a model for *single* measurements (e.g., collections of ACT scores, IQ scores, etc.). However, our question above is not one about *single* measurements. We are not interested in the likelihood of a *single person* scoring 25 or above – instead, we are interested in the likelihood of 10 individuals getting a *mean* ACT score of

DOI: 10.4324/9781003181828-4

25 or above. This is a different question altogether. To answer it, we must learn how to model *sample means*, not just individual scores.

Modeling sample means

If we want to compare how well our sample of 10 students performed on the ACT compared to the general population, we need a good model for the **distribution of sample means** that we would expect when 10 people take the ACT. In other words, when we take samples of size $N = 10$ from our population of test takers, what sample means do we expect? Is a sample mean of $\bar{X} = 25$ very likely to occur?

To answer this, I want to take a step back and consider a much simpler problem. Instead of taking samples of ACT scores and computing their means, let's roll a pair of dice and compute the mean of the two rolls. Here, the population of "scores" I can get from rolling a die is very small – the only possible outcomes are the whole numbers 1, 2, 3, 4, 5, 6. Thus, there are only finitely many "samples" of size $N = 2$ that I can obtain. For example, if I rolled a 1 and a 3, the sample mean would be $\bar{X} = (1+3)/2 = 2$. Similarly, if I rolled a 2 and a 5, the sample mean would be $\bar{X} = (2+5)/2 = 3.5$. In fact, I can systematically calculate *every possible* sample mean that I could obtain in this experiment – the results are in the table below:

	1	2	3	4	5	6
1	1	1.5	2	2.5	3	3.5
2	1.5	2	2.5	3	3.5	4
3	2	2.5	3	3.5	4	4.5
4	2.5	3	3.5	4	4.5	5
5	3	3.5	4	4.5	5	5.5
6	3.5	4	4.5	5	5.5	6

Close inspection of this table of sample means reveals that the only possible outcomes are the numbers 1, 1.5, 2, 2.5,...,5.5, 6. Also, these outcomes don't occur equally often. Numbers in the middle of this range like 3 and 3.5 occur much more often than the numbers on the ends, like 1 and 6. In fact, we can calculate the probability of every outcome exactly. As there are 36 possible means displayed in the table, the probability of obtaining a sample mean of 1 is exactly $1/36 = 0.028$, whereas the probability of obtaining a sample mean of 3.5 is $6/36 = 0.167$. Figure 4.1 shows a plot of this probability distribution, giving each possible sample mean along with its probability (i.e., relative frequency).

Figure 4.1 displays not only the two properties that we already noticed (i.e., that means of 1 and 6 are quite unlikely, whereas a mean of 3.5 is the most likely outcome) but also some other interesting patterns. First, notice the symmetry of the distribution around the peak at 3.5. A sample mean of 4.0 has

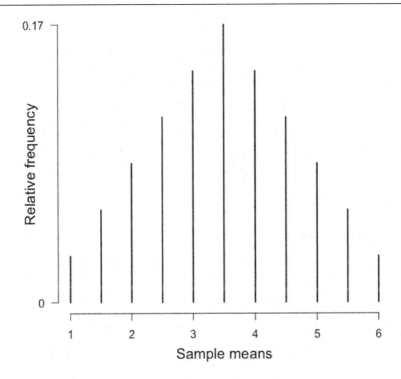

Figure 4.1 Distribution of means for samples of two dice.

exactly the same probability as 3.0, and this pattern continues as we progress away from 3.5. While this distribution is not a normal distribution, it does seem to have some of the same visual properties.

Of course, in our example with ACT scores, we had a sample of $N = 10$, which is probably quite a different situation. So, what happens as we increase the *sample size* in our dice experiment? This is an easy experiment to conduct: simply throw *three* dice. Suppose we get the three numbers 1, 1, and 4 – then the sample mean would be $\bar{X} = (1+1+4)/3 = 2$. What are all the possible outcomes? This time, it is a little more difficult to write them down – whereas with two dice we had 36 possible outcomes, this time there are 216 possibilities! But just like with samples of size $N = 2$, the possibilities only range between 1 and 6. Also, it is no problem for a computer to tabulate all the possibilities. In fact, in Figure 4.2 below, I have plotted the possible means (and their associated relative frequencies) for samples of size $N = 3$, $N = 4$, $N = 5$, and $N = 6$. Take a close look at the distributions in Figure 4.2, and you should notice something very striking!

As you can see, the distributions remain symmetric around a sample mean of 3.5, but the shape as you move away from 3.5 toward the ends becomes sort of curvy. In fact, it really is starting to look a lot like a normal distribution.

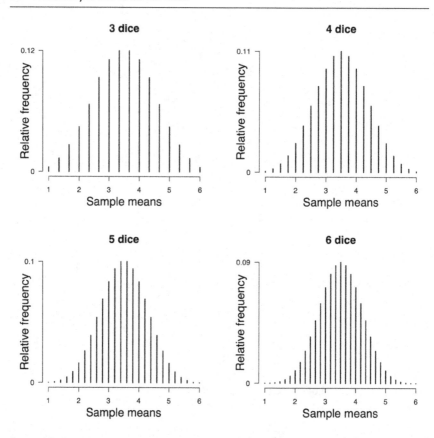

Figure 4.2 Distributions of sample means for rolls of N = 3, 4, 5, 6 dice, respectively.

Could it really be the case that the distribution of sample means is a normal distribution? If so, that would explain a lot of the reason that we talked about it so much in Chapter 3!

Let's try something else. This time, instead of using dice we'll simulate some different *population models*; that is, randomly generated data points that follow a specific probability distribution. In the top row of Figure 4.3 below, you'll see histograms of three such distributions, each constructed in the software package R by randomly generating 1,000,000 measurements which have a mean of 50 and a standard deviation of 16 (the specific numbers aren't impor-tant right now – just that they're consistent across the different randomly gen-erated datasets). The data in the leftmost histogram were generated from a normal distribution; notice that the histogram roughly follows the shape of a normal distribution. The data in the center histogram were generated from a uniform distribution; though it is not perfectly flat, it does roughly follow the rectangular shape of a uniform distribution. Finally, the data in the rightmost

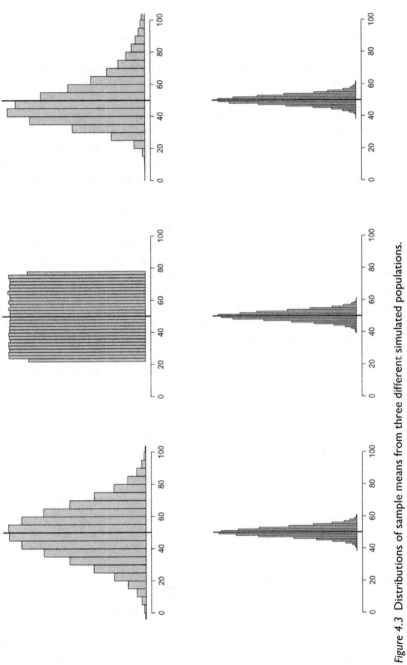

Figure 4.3 Distributions of sample means from three different simulated populations.

histogram were generated from a skewed distribution (specifically, something called the ex-Gaussian distribution).

After generating the populations, I then constructed distributions of sample means for each population. Again, I did this in R with a simulation, where I repeatedly drew samples of size $N = 30$ and computed the sample mean – 1,000 times in total. Then I constructed a histogram of these 1,000 means. The distribution of sample means is placed directly below the population from which it was derived. Notice the striking similarity of the three distributions in the bottom of Figure 4.3. And, just like our dice example above in Figure 4.2, the distributions of sample means are symmetric around a central value (this time, 50). They really seem to look a lot like normal distributions.

But there's even more going on in Figure 4.3. First, notice that *each* distribution of sample means is centered at a mean of 50 – just like the original population from which it was derived. This says that, on average, the means of the samples tend to be close to the original population mean. Second, compared to the original populations in the top row, the sample means are very tightly clustered around the mean. This should make some sense, especially when the original population is normally distributed – the most likely values to be sampled are close to 50, whereas values much larger and/or smaller than 50 are less likely to have been selected in the sample. But remarkably, this even holds for the uniform distribution (middle column). The same argument cannot be applied here, as each possible measurement is *equally likely* to be sampled. Nonetheless, the distribution of sample means follows the same shape – normally distributed, centered at 50, and much less variable than the original population.

The intuition we've gained from this remarkable picture can actually be formalized as a mathematical principle called the **central limit theorem**. Any reader wanting a rigorous mathematical treatment of the central limit theorem can consult a textbook on mathematical statistics or probability theory (e.g., Hoel, 1984; Larson, 1995; Pruim, 2018). A technical presentation of this principle is beyond the scope of the book, but in its most basic form, the central limit theorem says the following:

Consider a distribution with given mean μ and standard deviation σ. Suppose we take samples of size N. Then the distribution of sample means has the following properties:

1 *it is approximately normal;*
2 *it has mean equal to μ;*
3 *it has standard deviation equal to $\sigma / \sqrt{N}$.*

This is an absolutely remarkable fact! In plain terms, it says that no matter what model we place on the population of measurements that we care about, the *sample means* will always form a distribution that is well-described by a normal distribution with mean μ and standard deviation $\sigma / \sqrt{N}$. Note that the approximation to the normal distribution gets better as the sample size increases, though we can see from Figure 4.3 that $N = 30$ is sufficient to produce a distribution of sample means that is indistinguishable from a typical normal distribution.

Before moving on to some examples, I'll mention that the standard deviation of the distribution of sample means is often given a special name – the **standard error of the mean**, or *SE* for short. Whenever you see the phrase **standard error** in the rest of the book, this is simply another name for the standard error of the distribution of sample means. I don't know about you, but I'd much rather use the phrase "standard error".

Using the central limit theorem

We are now ready to go back to the motivating problem that we encountered early on in this chapter. Recall that we have implemented a semester-long training intervention that is designed to help students score as high as possible on the ACT. At the conclusion of the program, we had a sample of $N = 10$ students take the ACT, and their mean score was $\overline{X} = 25$. We would like to know something about how *this* sample performed compared to all other possible samples of size 10.

One specific question we might ask is about **percentile rank** – that is, what proportion of samples would score below our obtained mean of $\overline{X} = 25$? In symbols, we want to know $P(\overline{X} < 25)$.

To compute the proportion, we need to know what the distribution of all possible sample means for samples of size $N = 10$ looks like. Fortunately, the central limit theorem tells us everything we need to know.

- The distribution of sample means is approximately *normal.*
- The mean of the distribution of sample means is the same as the original population. For ACT scores, this is $\mu = 21$.
- The standard error (i.e., the standard deviation of the distribution of sample means) is equal to the standard deviation of the original population divided by the square root of the sample size. For ACT scores, we have $\sigma = 6$, so the standard error is

$$
\begin{aligned}
SE &= \frac{\sigma}{\sqrt{N}} \\
&= \frac{6}{\sqrt{10}} \\
&= \frac{6}{3.16} \\
&= 1.90.
\end{aligned}
$$

Recall that any problem involving proportions/probabilities can be easily solved by transforming everything to z-scores. We'll do that here and convert our sample mean $\bar{X} = 25$ to a z-score:

$$z = \frac{\bar{X} - \mu}{SE}$$

$$= \frac{25 - 21}{1.90}$$

$$= \frac{4}{1.90}$$

$$= 2.11.$$

Thus, we can find $P(\bar{X} < 25)$ by finding instead $P(z < 2.11)$ on the standard normal distribution, which we can use the PsyStat app to compute (https://tomfaulkenberry.shinyapps.io/psystat). As can be seen in Figure 4.4, the

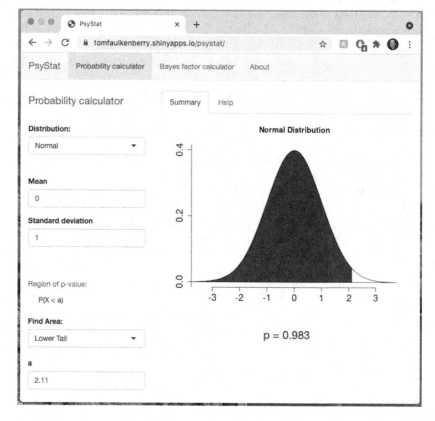

Figure 4.4 Screenshot of the PsyStat app.

PsyStat app gives us a proportion of $p = 0.983$, which means that our sample (which received the training) had an average ACT score better than 98.3% of all possible samples of size 10.

More practice

It would be easy to stop here and move on to the next chapter, but we need a little more practice with these concepts in order to fully appreciate the subtlety involved in our discussion of the central limit theorem and what it says about modeling observed data. To motivate this discussion, let's consider a new example. Suppose we have a standardized mathematics test whose scores form a normal distribution with mean $\mu = 70$ and standard deviation $\sigma = 10$. Let's consider three different questions that we could ask about this test:

1   What proportion of scores will be less than $X = 75$?
2   If samples of size $N = 4$ are selected at random from the population, what proportion of the samples will have means less than $\bar{X} = 75$?
3   If samples of size $N = 25$ are selected at random from the population, what proportion of the samples will have means less than $\bar{X} = 75$?

Before answering these questions, I want you to stop and think about how the answers relate to each other. What does your gut tell you?

Let's think about this conceptually first. Each question is of a similar nature – it asks to compute the proportion of *something* that is less than 75. For the first question, that "something" is scores; for the second and third questions, that "something" is *sample means*. Thus, these questions will be answered by considering fundamentally different models of the underlying objects. For Question 1, we will simply use a normal distribution, as we already know that the test was designed so that the scores follow such a distribution. For Question 2, we're interested not in scores, but in sample means that come from samples of size $N = 4$. Thus, we'll need to use an appropriate model for sample means. Fortunately, the central limit theorem tells us that the means from samples of size N are well-modeled by a normal distribution with mean equal to μ (the original population mean) and standard deviation equal to $\sigma / \sqrt{N}$ (where σ is the standard deviation of the original population). Since the sample size is different for Questions 2 and 3, the underlying standard deviations of the distributions of sample means (i.e., the standard errors) will also be different. To this point, for Question 2 we will use a normal distribution with mean $\mu = 70$ and standard deviation equal to $10 / \sqrt{4} = 10 / 2 = 5$. But for Question 3, the normal distribution (with mean $\mu = 70$) will have standard deviation $10 / \sqrt{25} = 10 / 5 = 2$.

I have attempted to visually depict the fundamental differences between these distributions in Figure 4.5. In each plot, I have shaded the region corresponding to values less than 75, but notice how the regions are drastically

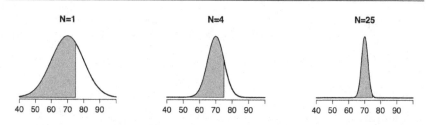

Figure 4.5 Proportion of sample means less than 75 for three different sample sizes.

different. As the central limit theorem predicts, the width (i.e., the standard deviation) of the normal distribution decreases as the sample size increases. Thus, with a fixed region (i.e., $P(X < 75)$), the relative proportion of the curve that corresponds to this region will increase. To see what I mean, consider how things change as I move from left to right in Figure 4.5. In the leftmost plot (where we are modeling single scores; i.e., $N = 1$), the gray region corresponding to scores less than 75 is just a little more than half of the normal curve. There is still an appreciable amount that is greater than 75. In the middle plot, the gray region corresponding to having a sample mean less than 75 (where the sample size is $N = 4$) may look like a smaller region, but as a proportion it is actually a much larger area. This pattern continues in the rightmost plot, where the gray region corresponding to sample means less than 75 (where the sample size is $N = 25$) is almost all of the normal curve.

Against this conceptual background, let's compute the exact proportions for each of these questions. As before, we'll convert each of the observed scores into z-scores and use the PsyStat app.

1   To compute the proportion of scores less than $X = 75$, we simply convert $X = 75$ to a z-score. We simply need to know that the mean of the distribution of scores is $\mu = 70$ and the standard deviation is $\sigma = 10$. This gives us

$$z = \frac{X - \mu}{\sigma}$$
$$= \frac{75 - 70}{10}$$
$$= \frac{5}{10}$$
$$= 0.5.$$

Thus, $P(X < 75)$ is equivalent to $P(z < 0.5)$. From here, we can use PsyStat to compute $P(z < 0.5)$; choose "Lower tail" and set $a = 0.5$ to get $p = 0.691$, which tells us that 69.1% of the test scores are less than 75.

2 To compute the proportion of *sample means* (where $N = 4$) that are less than $\bar{X} = 75$, we can again convert $\bar{X} = 75$ to a z-score. But this time, we need to consider that the standard deviation of the distribution of sample means (i.e., the standard error) is $SE = \sigma / \sqrt{N} = 10 / \sqrt{4} = 10 / 2 = 5$. This yields

$$z = \frac{\bar{X} - \mu}{SE}$$
$$= \frac{75 - 70}{5}$$
$$\overset{\cdot}{=} \frac{5}{5}$$
$$= 1.$$

This time, note that $P(\bar{X} < 75)$ is the same thing as $P(z < 1)$. As above, we can use PsyStat; with "Lower tail" and $a = 1$, we get $p = 0.841$. This means that 84.1% of the sample means (where $N = 4$) are less than 75. Compared to Question 1, this says something that you might have already noticed. It is much more likely to get a sample mean less than 75 ($p = 0.841$) than to get a single score less than 75 ($p = 0.691$).

3 Finally, when $N = 25$, we proceed exactly as in Question 2, but this time the standard error is $SE = \sigma / \sqrt{N} = 10 / \sqrt{25} = 10 / 5 = 2$. This gives us

$$z = \frac{\bar{X} - \mu}{SE}$$
$$= \frac{75 - 70}{2}$$
$$= \frac{5}{2}$$
$$= 2.5.$$

This tells us that for samples of size $N = 25$, $P(\bar{X} < 75)$ is the same thing as $P(z < 2.5)$. From PsyStat, you should get $p = 0.994$, which indicates that 99.4% of the sample means will be less than 75 when we have a sample size of $N = 25$.

So, what is the broader lesson of these examples? One important implication is that as sample size increases, it becomes harder and harder get sample means that are significantly far away from the population mean. As we just saw, for $N = 25$ the proportion of sample means less than 75 (i.e, 5 points above the population mean) is 99.4%. Said differently, this means that the proportion of sample means *greater* than 75 (i.e., greater than 5 points above the population mean) is only 0.6%. In terms of probability, this means that it is very unlikely (i.e., $p = 0.006$) that your sample mean will be this far away from the population mean.

Looking ahead

Why does all this matter? After all, why do we care about distributions of sample means and these proportions and probabilities? Well, suppose you made some hypothesis about some unknown population mean. For example, let's consider a scenario where you wanted to test whether some instructional program made an impact on these standardized math test scores. So, you randomly select $N = 25$ students to go through this instructional program, and then subsequently assess them with the standardized math test. You know that for the general population, the mean score is 70. Let's play devil's advocate – if your instructional program had *no impact*, you would expect your experimental sample to have a mean close to 70. After all, we know from our work in this chapter that sample means do not deviate far from the population mean, especially as sample size increases. But you observe a sample mean of $\overline{X} = 75$. How likely is this observed data, under the assumption that the instructional program had no impact. From what we just did, we know that we are very unlikely to have gotten a score of 75 or greater under such an assumption (specifically, we know that this probability is $p = 0.006$.) So, maybe it is the case that our assumption of no impact is incorrect.

You might need to read that paragraph again, because it is foreshadowing an important way of reasoning that we are about to describe in the next chapter. I'll leave the details there, but the basic idea is that we can reason about the impact of our instructional program by arguing that it could *not* be the case that the program did *not* work. In a sense, we are applying a double negative – "there's not no effect". While this sentence is certainly a grammatical disaster, it distills the basic logic of **null hypothesis testing**, a classical technique for assessing whether there are **statistically significant** differences that result from experimental treatments.

By the way, don't put the book down at this point and tell everyone that I told you that it was OK to use double negatives. I am simply trying to illustrate a point. Let's go forward and read Chapter 5 – arguably one of the most important chapters in this book. It is there that I will finally describe (in detail) one of the big things that we do most often in psychological statistics.

Chapter summary

This chapter was a very important one! Let's summarize what we've learned:

1 Observed data in psychological research is often in the form of *sample means*, not single measurements.

2 To find out what specific values of sample means are expected, we need to be able to build a *distribution of sample means.*

3 We saw that when we take larger and larger samples, the shape of the distribution of the sample means begins to look more and more like a normal distribution.

4 The *central limit theorem* tells us that our intuition in summary point #3 is correct – it is a mathematical principle which says that the distribution of sample means:

- – is approximately a normal distribution,
- – has mean equal to the mean of the original distribution of scores/ measurements (i.e., μ), and
- – has standard deviation equal to the standard deviation of the original distribution divided by the square root of the sample size (i.e., $\sigma / \sqrt{N}$). This standard deviation is sometimes called the *standard error.*

5 We can use the central limit theorem to convert any given sample mean into a z-score, which allows us to use the PsyStat calculator to compute proportions and probabilities associated with the sample mean.

Supplementary video lecture

If you would like to watch an online video lecture where I discuss the concepts we talked about in this chapter, you can navigate your web browser to https://youtu.be/80ngZHOHTZA. In this video, I walk through some different simulations to develop the central limit theorem, so this might afford you an even better understanding of how distributions of sample means work.

Exercises

1 Suppose you have a collection of scores that is normally distributed with $\mu = 60$ and $\sigma = 15$, and suppose we randomly draw samples of size $N = 25$.

   a   What proportion of the samples will have means greater than 63?
   b   What proportion of the samples will have means less than 54?
   c   What proportion of the samples will have a mean between 59 and 61?

2 For a normal population with $\mu = 400$ and $\sigma = 30$,

   a   What is the probability of obtaining a sample mean greater than 405 for a random sample of $N = 9$ scores?
   b   What is the probability of obtaining a sample mean greater than 405 for a random sample of $N = 25$ scores?
   c   For a sample of $N = 36$ scores, what is the probability that the sample mean will be within 3 points of the population mean?

3 The population of intelligence test scores forms a normal distribution with a mean of $\mu = 100$ and a standard deviation of $\sigma = 15$. What is the probability of obtaining a sample mean greater than $\bar{X} = 98$,

a   for a random sample of $N = 16$ people?
b   for a random sample of $N = 49$ people?

4 At the end of the semester, the Associate Dean sends a survey to all new faculty members in the college. One question asked the faculty members how much weight they had gained or lost since the beginning of term. Over the past several years, the average has been a gain of $\mu = 5.2$ pounds with a standard deviation of $\sigma = 4.8$ pounds. The distribution of scores was approximately normal. This semester, a sample of $N = 6$ new faculty members were selected and the average weight change was computed for the sample.

a   What is the probability that the sample mean will be greater than 8 pounds?
b   Among all possible samples, what proportion will *lose* weight?
c   What is the probability that the sample mean will be a gain of between 8 and 10 pounds?

Chapter 5

Comparing statistical models

In Chapter 1, I argued that the goal in psychological statistics is to *compare models* of human behavior. After gaining some background knowledge in Chapters 2–4, we are now ready to attack this goal. Let's learn how to compare statistical models of our observed data.

As a working example, let's consider a scenario that will look quite familiar after reading the last chapter. Suppose we are measuring mathematical skill with a standardized mathematics assessment called the TMA (Test for Mathematical Achievement). The test developers have designed this assessment to have a mean of 70 and a standard deviation of 10. We are particularly interested in testing the efficacy of a new mathematics instructional program. To this end, we have recruited a random sample of $N = 25$ people to go through the program. After the program has ended, we then measure the participants' mathematics skill with the TMA, and we find that the mean score for our sample is $\bar{X} = 75$. From this observed data, we then ask the obvious question: *Did the instructional program work?*

To answer this, we need to translate the research question into a *statistical question*. Let μ represent the mean TMA score of the population who receive the instructional program. If the instructional program worked, then this population mean should be greater than the mean test score for the general population. That is, we should see that $\mu > 70$. With this in mind, we can directly translate the research question "Did the instructional program work?" into a simply stated statistical question: *Is $\mu > 70$?*

The difficulty here lies with the fact that μ is an *unobservable* quantity. We cannot possibly administer the instructional program to every person and then measure their mathematics skill with the TMA. The only thing we can do is to observe a sample from this population, and then use the sample to make an *inference* about μ. Here, we will describe two methods for making this inference:

1 we can **estimate** the value of μ directly from our sample mean $\bar{X}$;
2 we can perform a **model comparison** (or **hypothesis test**), which lets us directly compare two models of μ.

DOI: 10.4324/9781003181828-5

Method 1 – Estimating μ from $\bar{X}$

At first pass, there might seem to be an obvious way to estimate the value of the population mean μ – just use the *sample mean* $\bar{X}$. This is absolutely a good idea, but restricting our estimate of μ to a single value ignores the inherent variability that is present when we sample from a population. If you think back to our discussion of distributions of sample means from Chapter 4, you'll remember that when you take a sample from a population with mean μ, the most likely value for the sample mean $\bar{X}$ is indeed μ. But we cannot be certain about the exact value of our specific sample mean $\bar{X}$. Thus, our method of estimation must factor in this uncertainty.

Let's walk through a classic way to do this. We know from Chapter 4 that the distribution of sample means from this population is approximately a normal distribution with mean equal to the mean of the population (i.e., μ) and standard deviation (i.e., standard error) equal to $SE = \sigma / \sqrt{N}$, where σ is the standard deviation of the population and N is the sample size. Further, we know from our discussion of normal distributions in Chapter 3 that approximately 95% of the values in a normal distribution will be within two standard deviations of the mean (actually, the value that gives almost exactly 95% is 1.96). Thus, 95% of the sample means $\bar{X}$ will be within two *standard errors* of μ (see Figure 5.1).

In terms of probability, this implies that there is a 95% probability that any given sample mean will be between the left endpoint of $\mu - 1.96 \cdot SE$ and the right endpoint of $\mu + 1.96 \cdot SE$. We can write this mathematically (replacing the standard error term SE with $\sigma / \sqrt{N}$) as a compound inequality:

$$\mu - 1.96 \cdot \frac{\sigma}{\sqrt{N}} < \bar{X} < \mu + 1.96 \cdot \frac{\sigma}{\sqrt{N}}.$$

Distribution of sample means

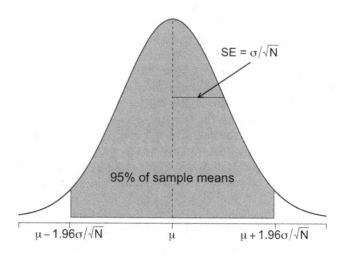

Figure 5.1 A visual representation of how 95% of the possible sample means lie within 1.96 standard errors of the mean.

Since our goal is to estimate μ, let's try to get μ in the middle of this inequality – doing so would give us a range of values that could bound μ. It takes a little bit of algebra, but the interested reader can verify that the inequality converts to:

$$\overline{X}-1.96\cdot\frac{\sigma}{\sqrt{N}}<\mu<\overline{X}+1.96\cdot\frac{\sigma}{\sqrt{N}}.$$

Let's interpret this inequality in words – those symbols mean that we are 95% confident that μ is between a lower bound of $\overline{X}-1.96\sigma/\sqrt{N}$ and an upper bound of $\overline{X}+1.96\sigma/\sqrt{N}$. We take this inequality as a definition for a **confidence interval**.

---

*Definition: A 95% **confidence interval (CI)** for estimating an unknown population mean from a sample mean $\overline{X}$ is given by the interval:*

$$\left(\overline{X}-1.96\cdot\frac{\sigma}{\sqrt{N}},\overline{X}+1.96\cdot\frac{\sigma}{\sqrt{N}}\right).$$

Note that in this approach, we are assuming that the value of the population standard deviation σ does not change as a result of the intervention. Using the context of our example, this means we are assuming that the instructional program does not affect the variability of the scores – only the center.

Back to our example: we want to know if $\mu>70$, which would mean that the mean mathematics achievement score after the instructional program is larger than the mean score for the general population. Since μ is unknown, let's estimate it with a confidence interval. For our sample of size $N=25$, we observed a mean of $\overline{X}=75$. Also, recall that $\sigma=10$. Thus, we can compute:

$$CI=\left(\overline{X}-1.96\cdot\frac{\sigma}{\sqrt{N}},\overline{X}+1.96\cdot\frac{\sigma}{\sqrt{N}}\right)$$

$$=\left(75-1.96\cdot\frac{10}{\sqrt{25}},75+1.96\cdot\frac{10}{\sqrt{25}}\right)$$

$$=\left(75-1.96\cdot\frac{10}{5},75+1.96\cdot\frac{10}{5}\right)$$

$$=\left(75-1.96\cdot 2,75+1.96\cdot 2\right)$$

$$=\left(75-3.92,75+3.92\right)$$

$$=\left(71.08,78.92\right)$$

Thus, we are 95% confident that the population mean μ is between 71.08 and 78.92. Since the entire range of our estimate is greater than 70 (the mean of the test for the general population), we can conclude that the instructional program did in fact increase mathematics skill.

Method 2 – Comparing models of μ

Whereas we used Method 1 to answer our research question by estimating the value of μ via a confidence interval, with Method 2 we take a different, albeit complementary approach. Remember that μ (which represents the mean math score after the instructional program) is unknown, so we would like to use our data to make some inference about μ. This time, we construct *models* (or *hypotheses*) about μ and compare them against the observed data; that is, which model is best supported by the data we observed. Classically, we do this by defining *two* models:

- a **null model** $\mathcal{H}_0 : \mu = 70$ – under this model, the instructional program did not work, as the mean score after the instructional program is the same as the mean score for the general population;
- an **alternative model** $\mathcal{H}_1 : \mu > 70$ – under this model, the instructional program *did* work, as the mean score after the instructional program is *greater* than that of the general population.

After defining these models, we want to compare them. Conceptually, this is a simple idea – *which model best predicts our observed data?* If the observed data are best predicted is the alternative model $\mathcal{H}_1$, then we can infer that our instructional program worked, because the defining characteristic of $\mathcal{H}_1$ is that μ is greater than the general population mean of 70. If, on the other hand, the observed data are best predicted by the null model $\mathcal{H}_0$, then we can infer that our instructional program had no effect on math scores, because the defining characteristic of this model is that μ is still equal to 70.

So how do we perform this model comparison? It turns out that this simple question is so fundamental that its answer defines the *type* of statistics we are performing. Let's consider one possible method for doing this model comparison. We could compute the probability of observing the data under $\mathcal{H}_0$. That is, what is the probability of getting a sample mean $\overline{X} = 75$ if $\mu = 70$? Then we could compute the probability of observing the same data under $\mathcal{H}_1$. That is, what is the probability of getting a sample mean $\overline{X} = 75$ if $\mu > 70$? Once we've done that, we would simply choose the model with the largest of these probabilities. Sounds easy, right?

It turns out that this method, while conceptually simple, is mathematically quite difficult to implement. Without getting into too many details,

I'll mention that the problem lies with the second of these probabilities. Computing the probability of observing $\bar{X} = 75$ under $\mathcal{H}_0$ involves only *one* value for μ (i.e., $\mu = 70$), which just involves a simple calculation with a normal distribution, just as we did in Chapter 3. But computing the probability of observing $\bar{X} = 75$ under $\mathcal{H}_1$ involves a *range* of values for μ (remember, $\mathcal{H}_1$ assumes $\mu > 70$). This is more difficult, as there are an infinite number of possible values for μ, each with a different *a priori* probability. Such computations are the hallmark of something called *Bayesian statistics*, which we will come back to in Chapter 7.

So instead of taking this approach to model comparison, I will propose one that may seem conceptually more difficult but is mathematically easier to perform. Here's how it works. Let's start by assuming that the null model $\mathcal{H}_0$ is *true*. If so, then we are assuming from the beginning that $\mu = 70$. From here, we will then compute the probability of observing our data ($\bar{X} = 75$) under this assumption. Two things can happen:

1 If this probability is small (say, less than 5%), this means that the data we observed are *rare* under $\mathcal{H}_0$ – that is, those data shouldn't have happened.
2 If this probability is not small (say, greater than 5%), this means that the data we observed are reasonably plausible under $\mathcal{H}_0$.

Let's consider each of these outcomes. Under the first outcome, we see that our actually observed data quite simply should not have happened – if the null model $\mathcal{H}_0 : \mu = 70$ were true. But they did – after all, we *observed* the data $\bar{X} = 75$. Logically, this implies that our original *assumption* was incorrect. That is, we *reject* the assumption that $\mu = 70$. Rejecting this null model leaves us with support (albeit indirect) for the competing model $\mathcal{H}_1 : \mu > 70$. From this, we can conclude that the instructional program worked.

Under the second outcome, we see that our observed data are reasonably plausible under the null model $\mathcal{H}_0 : \mu = 70$. That is, even though we obtained a sample mean math score of 75, such a score would be reasonably likely to occur even if the post-instruction population mean math score μ is still only $\mu = 70$. In this case, our inference is that the instructional program had no effect (i.e., it did not work as desired).

If this is beginning to get confusing, do not worry. We will go through this procedure many times throughout this and the next chapter. In fact, let's now walk through our guiding example and see what actually happens.

Remember, our goal is to compute the probability of observing our data *if the null model is true*. In symbols, we want to compute $p = P(\text{data} \mid \mathcal{H}_0)$. So, let's start with the assumption that $\mathcal{H}_0$ is true (i.e., $\mu = 70$). Our goal is to compute the probability of getting a sample mean $\bar{X}$ at least as extreme as the one we observed: $p = P(\bar{X} \geq 75)$. This should seem familiar, as we just encountered this type of question in the previous chapter. Recall that we first convert the observed sample mean to a z-score. From Chapter 4, we see:

$$
\begin{aligned}
z &= \frac{\bar{X} - \mu}{SE} \\
&= \frac{\bar{X} - \mu}{\sigma / \sqrt{N}} \\
&= \frac{75 - 70}{10 / \sqrt{25}} \\
&= \frac{5}{10 / 5} \\
&= \frac{5}{2} \\
&= 2.5.
\end{aligned}
$$

Note the importance of our assumption that $\mu = 70$. Without this assumption, we would not have been able to compute this z-score, as μ is an unknown population parameter. But with the assumption, the calculation proceeds nicely.

Now that we have recast our probability $p = P(\bar{X} \geq 75)$ into a z-score probability $p = P(z \geq 2.5)$, we can use the PsyStat app to easily compute it. That is,

$$
\begin{aligned}
p &= P(\bar{X} \geq 75) \\
&= P(z \geq 2.5) \\
&= 0.00621.
\end{aligned}
$$

As you can see, this probability is very small (certainly less than 5%), so this tells us that observing a sample mean of $\bar{X} = 75$ is very unlikely if $\mu = 70$. This calls into question our original assumption of the null model $\mathcal{H}_0 : \mu = 70$, as we have actually observed that sample mean. Thus, we reject the null model $\mathcal{H}_0$ in favor of the alternative model $\mathcal{H}_1 : \mu > 70$, and hence conclude that the population mean score of the math test after the instructional program is indeed greater than 70. The instructional program worked!

Another example

Unfortunately, one example is not enough to truly understand what is going on in this chapter, so we will work together through another example now.

But, before doing so, let me attempt to quickly summarize what we've learned so far.

1 Estimation works by constructing a 95% confidence interval for μ. That is, we use the sample mean and the population standard deviation (along with the sample size) to mathematically calculate an interval which we are reasonably confident contains the unknown value of μ.

2 Model comparison (also known as hypothesis testing) works by comparing how well the observed data are predicted by two competing models (a null model and an alternative model). We assume the null is true (i.e., μ is equal to some specific context-dependent value) and calculate the probability of observing our sample mean (or more extreme) under this assumption. If this probability (called a **p-value**) is small – typically less than 5% – this tells us that our observed data are rare under the null. This implies that we should reject the null model and instead consider the alternative model as the "correct" model. On the other hand, if the p-value is larger than 5%, we conclude that the observed data could reasonably be expected under the null, so we conclude that the null is the correct model.

With this in mind, let's now consider a new example. Suppose we are interested in studying the effects of a specific computer game on players' fluid intelligence. For simplicity, let's assume that fluid intelligence scores in the general population are normally distributed with a mean of 100 and a standard deviation of 15. In our study, we measured fluid intelligence in a sample of $N = 64$ people who have played this computer game for a year or more. The sample had a mean fluid intelligence score of $\overline{X} = 102$. From this sample, can we conclude that players of this computer game have a significantly higher fluid intelligence score than the general population?

As above, we will approach this problem by converting the research question to a statistical question. Let μ represent the population mean fluid intelligence score for those people who have played this computer game for a year or more. Note that this is potentially different from 100, which is the population mean fluid intelligence score for the *general population* who may have or may not have played the computer game. Our research question then translates to the following statistical question: *Is $\mu > 100$?*

First, we will use the method of estimation to get a 95% confidence interval for μ. Recall that we construct a 95% confidence interval as:

$$\left(\overline{X} - 1.96 \cdot \frac{\sigma}{\sqrt{N}}, \overline{X} + 1.96 \cdot \frac{\sigma}{\sqrt{N}} \right)$$

where $\overline{X}$ is our observed sample mean (here, $\overline{X} = 102$), σ is the standard deviation of the underlying population (here, $\sigma = 15$), and N is the sample size (here, $N = 64$). Thus, our confidence interval looks like the following:

$$CI = \left(\bar{X} - 1.96 \cdot \frac{\sigma}{\sqrt{N}}, \bar{X} + 1.96 \cdot \frac{\sigma}{\sqrt{N}} \right)$$

$$= \left(102 - 1.96 \cdot \frac{15}{\sqrt{64}}, 102 + 1.96 \cdot \frac{15}{\sqrt{64}} \right)$$

$$= \left(102 - 1.96 \cdot \frac{15}{8}, 102 + 1.96 \cdot \frac{15}{8} \right)$$

$$= \left(102 - 1.96 \cdot 1.875, 102 + 1.96 \cdot 1.875 \right)$$

$$= \left(102 - 3.675, 102 + 3.675 \right)$$

$$= \left(98.325, 105.675 \right).$$

Thus, we are 95% confident that μ is between approximately 98.3 and 105.7. Note that the general population mean of 100 is included in this interval, so while it *could* be the case that μ is bigger than 100, there is a sizeable part of the interval where μ is less than 100. Thus, we cannot conclude from this estimate that $\mu > 100$, which calls into question the efficacy of the computer game at increasing fluid intelligence scores in its players.

Now let's work through a model comparison. To this end, let's define two models of μ. We define the null model as $\mathcal{H}_0 : \mu = 100$, which states that the population mean score among players is no different from 100, the population mean among the general population. We define the alternative model as $\mathcal{H}_1 : \mu > 100$, which states that the population mean score among players is *greater* than 100 (i.e., playing this computer game increases fluid intelligence). Let's compare these models against the observed data.

To do this, we first assume that the null model is correct – that is, $\mu = 100$. This allows us to compute the probability of obtaining our sample mean $\bar{X} = 102$ under the null. To compute probabilities, we need to transform our raw sample mean to a z-score:

$$z = \frac{\bar{X} - \mu}{SE}$$

$$= \frac{\bar{X} - \mu}{\sigma / \sqrt{N}}$$

$$= \frac{102 - 100}{15 / \sqrt{64}}$$

$$= \frac{2}{15 / 8}$$

$$= \frac{2}{1.875}$$

$$= 1.07.$$

Then, we can compute the p-value using our PsyStat app:

$$p = P(\overline{X} \geq 102)$$
$$= P(z \geq 1.07)$$
$$= 0.142.$$

Hence, the probability of observing our data under the null model is 0.142 (14.2%), which is certainly larger than 5%. That is, our observed data are reasonably plausible under the null model. So, we cannot reject the null model $\mathcal{H}_0 : \mu = 100$ as a reasonable model of μ. With this in mind, we cannot conclude that playing the computer game results in any appreciable increase of fluid intelligence score over the general population mean of 100.

One-tailed versus two-tailed model comparisons

In our previous examples, we asked research questions that were **directional**; that is, they were phrased to ask whether the mean of the treatment population was *greater* than some specific value. Said differently, we predicted that the treatment would *increase* scores relative to some general population. Similarly, any research question which asks whether the mean of the treatment population was *less* than some specific value (i.e., a decrease relative to the general population) would also be directional.

What if instead we wanted to know whether a treatment simply *changed* the mean of a treatment population? In this case, we would not have a specific direction to predict. Such **nondirectional** questions can also be translated to a statistical model. In our previous two examples, the p-value comes from one tail of the sampling distribution. In a nondirectional question, we need to consider *both tails* of our sampling distribution. For this reason, such nondirectional model comparisons are often called **two-tailed tests** (compared to **one-tailed tests** for directional models).

Let's modify our last example so that we can work through such a situation. Recall that in this problem, we are interested in whether playing a computer game impacts players' fluid intelligence scores, where fluid intelligence scores for the general population are normally distributed with mean 100 and standard deviation 15. In our sample of $N = 64$, we observed a mean fluid intelligence score of $\overline{X} = 102$. Is this significantly *different* from 100?

To answer this, we'll again define two models. The null model will look the same – $\mathcal{H}_0 : \mu = 100$. But this time, the alternative will look like this: $\mathcal{H}_1 : \mu \neq 100$. Mathematically, this formulation of $\mathcal{H}_1$ admits *two* possibilities – either $\mu > 100$ or $\mu < 100$.

From here, our model comparison proceeds exactly the same as before, up to a point. We assume $\mathcal{H}_0$ is correct, thus setting $\mu = 100$. We then convert our observed sample mean $\overline{X} = 102$ into a z-score. From before, we have already seen that this translates to $z = 1.07$. Now our goal is to see how likely such a z-score (or more extreme) would be if the null model is correct.

Here's where the procedure differs slightly from before. On one-tailed model comparisons, our p-value is defined to be the probability of observing a given z-score (or more extreme – *in the direction of the alternative model*). For a two-tailed comparison, there are *two* directions to consider under the alternative – either $\mu > 100$ or $\mu < 100$. Since our data translates to an observed z-score of $z = 1.07$, we must calculate the probability of obtaining either $z \geq 1.07$ or $z \leq -1.07$, as both inequalities reflect "more extreme" z-scores in the two directions specified under the alternative model. Notice that even though our observed z-score is positive, we specify -1.07 for the other direction, as -1.07 is equally far from 0 in the opposite direction.

Fortunately, it is still very easy to compute this two-tailed p-value. In PsyStat, we simply choose "Both Tails" in the "Find Area:" menu. Doing this will cause another entry field labeled "b" to appear. In the two numeric fields ("a" and "b"), we enter our two z-scores. Which one goes where? Notice the text under "Region of p-value" says $P(X < a$ or $X > b)$. This tells us that "a" should be -1.07 and "b" should be 1.07. In Figure 5.2, we can see that $p = 0.285$ – that is, there's a 28.5% chance that we could observe data as extreme as what we did under the null. This means that the null is still a plausible model of our observed data, and thus we cannot reject the null model.

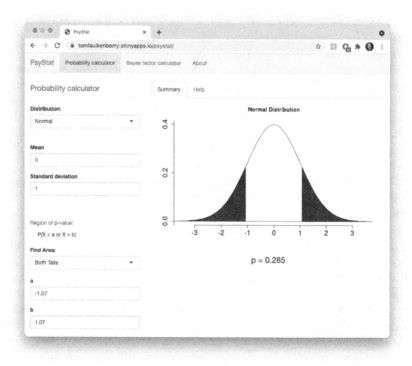

Figure 5.2 A screenshot of *PsyStat* demonstrating a two-tailed model comparison.

You might also notice that this p-value is twice the p-value we obtained from the one-tailed model comparison earlier. This will always happen. The reason is that the only thing we've changed is that we've added another tail to our sampling distribution, and because the sampling distribution is symmetric, the area of that second tail will exactly match the tail we already had, thus doubling the resulting p-value. Keep in mind that this p-value has no relation to the *size* of the effect – rather, it is simply the likelihood of observing our data (or more extreme) under the null hypothesis.

Estimation versus model comparison

Notice that in both examples above, the estimation procedure and the model comparison procedure gave identical answers to each research question. Are they redundant? Do we need to do both? I would argue that they are not completely redundant, and there is some benefit to doing both. Recently, there has been great debate in the psychological methods community about this very issue. Some researchers (e.g., Cumming, 2012; Cumming & Calin-Jageman, 2017) propose that estimation alone is sufficient to answer the kinds of questions psychologists are interested in answering. Still others (e.g., Morey et al., 2014; see also Wagenmakers et al., 2020) propose that *both* estimation and model comparison are essential for inference. While a full discussion of the relative merits of estimation and model comparison is beyond the scope of this book, I can offer some basic insight into this discussion.

I think the two procedures are complementary – when performing estimation, we construct a tangible range of values which we are reasonably confident contain the unknown population parameter μ. This is good in many contexts, as it gives a sense of the scale of any treatment effect that we might be considering. On the other hand, confidence intervals tend to be interpreted incorrectly. Technically the interval cannot be interpreted with a probability statement (i.e., "there is a 95% probability that μ is between X and Y"), but rather must be interpreted in a **frequentist** sense (i.e., out of 100 replications of this experiment, 95 of the constructed confidence intervals will contain the unknown value of μ). Admittedly, this is a difficult distinction to fully understand, which to me gives even more reason not to rely solely upon confidence intervals for inference.

A model comparison, on the other hand, can have its results interpreted as a probability. Whereas the result of an estimation procedure is a confidence interval, which cannot be interpreted as a probability, the main result of a model comparison is a p-value, which *is* a probability. Recall that the p-value is the probability of obtaining the observed sample mean (or more extreme) *if the null model is correct*. For example, if our model comparison gives us $p = 0.03$, this tells us that the probability of obtaining our actually observed sample mean is only 3% if the null model is correct. In other words, our data is rare under the null. But we did observe this sample mean! This calls into question the assumption that the null model is the correct one, so we reject the null model in favor of the alternative model.

Of course, this procedure for model comparison has some limitations. Chief among these is that evidence for the alternative model (i.e., the model which assumes a treatment effect) is only ever indirect. Look back at the logic we employ in the examples above. We never actually measure the probability of obtaining our sample mean under the alternative. Instead, our evidence for the alternative model only exists in the sense that the null model is not adequate. Note that there are ways to get around this, which we will discuss when I introduce Bayesian model comparison in Chapter 7. But for now, I will leave you with an anecdote that I always share in my introductory statistics courses. When we do model comparison in this manner, the way we conclude that there is a treatment effect is to conclude that "there is not no effect". I know that this statement is grammatically incorrect, but it is *conceptually* correct. We conclude in favor of the alternative by rejecting the null – literally, we are saying that it is "not" the case that there is "no effect".

Chapter summary

In a very real sense, you could stop reading now and jump into the world of psychological statistics. You've just learned two of the fundamental tools that are used in our discipline, regardless of the complexity of the data involved: confidence intervals and *p*-values. To recap,

1 A confidence interval is an interval of values which we are reasonably confident (usually 95% confident) contains some unknown population parameter (i.e., an unknown treatment mean).
2 A *p*-value is the probability of obtaining some observed data under a null model – that is, it indexes how *rare* the data is under the null. If the *p*-value is small (usually 5% is considered the threshold), we reject the null and instead choose the alternative model.

So, you may be wondering what could possibly be next? I'm glad you asked! It turns out that there is a fundamental assumption that I made throughout the previous discussion in this chapter – and it is hard to spot. I will discuss this issue in detail in the next chapter, but I can foreshadow it with a simple question. Regardless of whether we compute a confidence interval or a *p*-value, both calculations involve the population standard deviation σ. In both examples above, we knew the value of this standard deviation, because the examples used measures that were standardized to have fixed (known) values of σ. What happens when we are not given the value of σ?

I'll see you in Chapter 6, where we will figure out what to do in this situation.

Supplementary video lecture

If you would like to watch an online video lecture where I discuss the concepts we talked about in this chapter, you can navigate your web browser to https://youtu.be/7-I4GRbu-Q4.

Exercises

1 Suppose we are sampling from a population that is known to be normal with standard deviation $\sigma = 10$. However, the mean μ is unknown, so we'll have to estimate it.

   a   A sample of $N = 10$ is drawn and is found to have mean $\overline{X} = 25$. Compute a 95% confidence interval for μ.

   b   A sample of $N = 20$ is drawn and is also found to have mean $\overline{X} = 25$. Compute a 95% confidence interval for μ.

   c   Based on your answers to (a) and (b), what happens to the width of the confidence interval as sample size increases?

2 A treatment is administered to a sample of $N = 16$ individuals. The treatment population has unknown mean, but has a known standard deviation of $\sigma = 8$. The sample mean is found to be $\overline{X} = 33$.

   a   Compute a 95% confidence interval for μ, the mean of the treatment population.

   b   Define $\mathcal{H}_0 : \mu = 30$ and $\mathcal{H}_1 : \mu > 30$. What is the probability of observing a sample mean $\overline{X} = 33$ or larger if $\mathcal{H}_0$ is true?

   c   Given the results of (a) and (b), can we reject $\mathcal{H}_0$ in favor of $\mathcal{H}_1$? Why or why not?

3 A treatment is administered to a sample of $N = 25$ individuals. The treatment population has unknown mean, but has a known standard deviation of $\sigma = 5$. The sample mean is found to be $\overline{X} = 43$.

   a   Compute a 95% confidence interval for μ, the mean of the treatment population.

   b   Define $\mathcal{H}_0 : \mu = 40$ and $\mathcal{H}_1 : \mu > 40$. What is the probability of observing a sample mean $\overline{X} = 43$ or larger if $\mathcal{H}_0$ is true?

   c   Given the results of (a) and (b), can we reject $\mathcal{H}_0$ in favor of $\mathcal{H}_1$? Why or why not?

4 A professor has designed a new course intended to help students prepare for the verbal section of Graduate Record Exam (GRE). A sample of $N = 20$ students is recruited to take the course and, at the end of the year, each student takes the GRE. The average score for this sample is 155. For the general population, scores on the GRE are standardized to form a normal distribution with a mean of 150 and a standard deviation of 8.5. Can the professor conclude that students who take the course score significantly higher than the general population? Use the tools you've learned in this chapter to justify your answer.

Chapter 6

Introduction to the *t*-test

By reading the title of this chapter, you may be struck with a sense of familiarity. Maybe you've heard about *t*-tests before. But what exactly is a *t*-test, and how does it differ from what we've already done so far? I will answer that question in this chapter. To that end, let's begin with an example.

When I teach my introductory statistics course, I always give a standardized multiple-choice test at the end of the course. The purpose of this 100-question test is to assess how much my students have learned throughout the semester. Over the past several years, I have found that my students miss an average of 23 questions out of these 100. Not bad, but I'd like this number to be smaller. So, I made some modifications to my course. Since then, I've taught four different sections of the course, and the following scores represent the average numbers of errors that students from each of these sections made on the test:

20, 22, 22, 20.

Given these data, did the course modifications result in significantly better average end-of-course test scores (i.e., smaller numbers of errors)?

Immediately, we can easily compute the mean of our sample as

$$
\begin{aligned}
\bar{X} &= \frac{\sum X_i}{N} \\
&= \frac{20 + 22 + 22 + 20}{4} \\
&= \frac{84}{4} \\
&= 21.
\end{aligned}
$$

A mean score of 21 errors certainly seems better than the previous average of 23 errors that I was seeing before the modifications. Let's use the tools of the previous chapters and perform statistical inference on these data.

DOI: 10.4324/9781003181828-6

In perhaps an odd twist, this time we will perform a model comparison first (you'll see why a little later in this chapter). Let μ represent the mean of the *treatment population* – in this example, the population is the collection of all possible classes that could potentially use this redesigned statistics curriculum. Of course, we have no way to actually teach and test *all* of these classes, so we'll need to use my limited sample to infer things about this population mean μ. This way, we can generalize our results to other classes.

What we'll do is define and compare two models against these observed data. As we introduced in Chapter 5, these two models are:

- a null model $\mathcal{H}_0 : \mu = 23$: this model hypothesizes that the mean number of errors μ does not change after using the redesigned statistics curriculum;
- an alternative model $\mathcal{H}_1 : \mu < 23$: this model hypothesizes that the mean number of errors μ will *decrease* for classes that have used the redesigned statistics curriculum.

From here, you'll recall that we need to assume that the null model $\mathcal{H}_0$ is correct (i.e., we assume that $\mu = 23$), from which we then compute the probability of observing our data or more extreme (i.e., $\bar{X} \leq 21$). To compute this probability, we would need to convert the raw sample mean $\bar{X} = 21$ into a z-score:

$$z = \frac{\bar{X} - \mu}{\sigma / \sqrt{N}}.$$

Easy enough, except for one thing – we do not know a value for the population standard deviation σ. Indeed, in all previous examples we encountered back in Chapter 5, we could ascertain from context a value for σ to use. But in this case, all we know about the population is its mean μ (which by our assumption of $\mathcal{H}_0$ is equal to 23). We do not, on the other hand, have any such assumption about its standard deviation σ. So what do we do?

One straightforward way around this problem is simply to estimate its value from our observed data – that is, we compute the standard deviation of the four class averages (20, 22, 22, and 20). Recall from Chapter 2 that the standard deviation is roughly equal to the average amount that each data point differs from the mean. To compute this, we find the average of the squared deviations from the mean and take its square root; that is,

$$\text{Standard deviation} = \sqrt{\frac{\sum (X_i - \bar{X})^2}{N}}.$$

But before doing this, I need to mention a very important point. Remember, we are using this small sample (with $N = 4$) to *estimate* the population standard deviation σ. It turns out that computing the standard deviation of the sample and using this value to estimate σ is problematic – it systematically *underestimates* the actual true value of σ. In other words, our estimator is *biased*. Fortunately, it also turns out that there is a very easy way to correct this bias. Note that in the formula above, we divide by the sample size N. If instead we divided by $N - 1$, the resulting "average squared deviation" under the square root symbol would slightly increase in value (after all, when you divide by a smaller number, the quotient gets bigger). Amazingly, this simple tweak is sufficient to remove the bias.

With this in mind, we will compute our estimate of the population standard deviation σ. To distinguish between the "true" value of σ and our *estimate* of σ, we'll denote our estimate as $\hat{\sigma}$, which we read as "sigma hat". In light of this, we compute our estimate as:

$$\hat{\sigma} = \sqrt{\frac{\sum (X_i - \bar{X})^2}{N - 1}}.$$

Again, note that the only difference between this formula and the old one we mentioned immediately above is the $N - 1$ in the denominator of the fraction, and remember that the only reason we make this change is to ensure that our procedure for estimating population standard deviations σ from data is not biased. This is purely a technical thing, but it is an important one, as we'll see soon enough.

OK, with that out of the way, let's see how we do when trying to estimate σ from our observed data. As in Chapter 2, I like to compute standard deviation using a table. First, we compute the deviations of each of our measurements X_i from the observed mean $\bar{X} = 21$:

X_i	$X_i - \bar{X}$
20	−1
22	+1
22	+1
20	−1

Remember that deviation scores $X_i - \bar{X}$ will always add to 0, which we can verify easily. Strictly speaking, this step is never necessary, but always a good check (especially for more lengthy datasets). Now we'll square each of these deviations so that we can get rid of the negative signs:

X_i	$X_i - \bar{X}$	$(X_i - \bar{X})^2$
20	−1	1
22	+1	1
22	+1	1
20	−1	1

In Chapter 2, when we computed the variance, we simply found the average of those squared deviations. That is, we found the sum of the squared deviations (SS, which some people simply call "sum of squares") and divided by N. But from our discussion above, we now know that doing this will result in an estimate for the population variance that is a bit too small. So instead of dividing by N, we divide by one smaller ($N-1$):

$$\text{Variance} = \frac{SS}{N-1} = \frac{1+1+1+1}{4-1}$$
$$= \frac{4}{3}$$
$$= 1.333.$$

Finally, to put things back on the same scale as the original measurements, we take the square root of the variance, giving us the estimated standard deviation:

$$\hat{\sigma} = \sqrt{1.333}$$
$$= 1.15.$$

From here, it might be tempting to proceed with the steps we learned in Chapter 5. After all, the population standard deviation σ is all we needed to be able to compute a z-score, which we could then use with our PsyStat app to calculate the probability of observing our data (or more extreme) under the null model $\mathcal{H}_0$. However, as your reading of this chapter so far may have already foreshadowed, there is yet another problem that we will encounter, and it is much more fundamental. To explain it, I need to back up a little bit.

Remember from Chapter 4 that the reason we use the normal distribution so much in psychological statistics is because it is a very good model of the situations we most often encounter – namely, when we want to assess the likelihood of observing certain sample means. In fact, it is exactly the central limit theorem that we encountered in Chapter 4 which guarantees that under certain conditions, our distribution of sample means is pretty close to a normal distribution, regardless of how the original measurements are distributed. Further, when we standardize our sample means as z-scores on this distribution of sample means, the resulting distribution is always a standard normal distribution with mean 0 and standard deviation 1. Of course, this assumes that we know the value of of the population standard deviation σ.

When we don't know σ and instead estimate it as $\hat{\sigma}$ from the procedure above, the resulting distribution of standardized "z-scores" is no longer a normal distribution, but something else entirely. Intuitively, the reason for this stems from the fact that the adjustment we use to estimate $\hat{\sigma}$ (dividing by

$N - 1$ instead of N) depends entirely on the sample size N. Mathematically, the bias that we remove in the calculation of $\hat{\sigma}$ is smaller as N gets larger. Thus, the distribution of standardized scores depends on the sample size N. This means that we can no longer use the normal distribution to compute our p-values, but instead must use some other distribution. Moreover, the distribution we would use for $N = 4$ will be different from the distribution we would use for $N = 25$ (or any other sample size N, for that matter).

So, what do we do now?

Fortunately, the solution to this problem was worked out over 100 years ago.

Student's *t*-distribution

I always love to tell this story to my statistics students. In the early 1900s, an English statistician (and chemist, brewer, etc…) named William Sealy Gosset worked as the head experimental brewer at Guinness brewery. There, Gossett developed a number of new statistical methods in the design of experiments. In particular, he discovered a new method for performing statistical testing with small samples. Here, he worked out the details of the distributions of sample means of size N that arises from bias-corrected estimates, like the $\hat{\sigma}$ that we computed above. This work was then published in the journal *Biometrika* in 1908, but interestingly it was not published under his actual surname Gosset, but rather under the pseudonym "Student". The reason for this was that scientists who worked at Guinness were not allowed to publish their research under their own names. Since that time, the family of distributions that Gosset worked out the details for have become known as *Student's t-distribution*.

Let's dig a little deeper into **Student's *t*-distribution**. As I mentioned before, it is a *family* of distributions – that is, instead of being a single probability distribution (with only one curve, as the normal distribution has), Student's *t*-distribution is an infinite collection of distributions – that is, there is one unique distribution for each possible value of N. To see this, consider Figure 6.1.

In Figure 6.1, I have plotted two different examples of a *t*-distribution – one which arises from samples of size $N = 4$ (just like the sample in our leading example), and one which arises from larger samples of size $N = 25$. Note that they both share some of the characteristics of the standard normal distribution, particularly in terms of their single peak at 0 and their symmetric shape. However, they are certainly different distributions. For one thing, the curve for $N = 4$ does not reach the same height at 0 as does the curve for $N = 25$. Along the same line, the tails of the $N = 4$ curve are "fatter" than those of the $N = 25$ curve. One immediate consequence of these differences is that we can no longer use the normal distribution in our PsyStat app to calculate probabilities. But fortunately, Student's *t*-distribution is built into the app too.

So, that's enough background – we are now ready to dive back into our problem. When we left it earlier, we had defined two models: a null model $\mathcal{H}_0 : \mu = 23$ and an alternative model $\mathcal{H}_1 : \mu < 23$. Further, we had found a

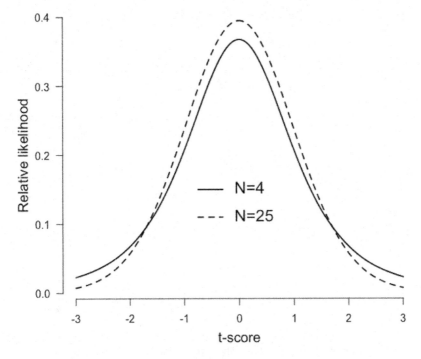

Figure 6.1 A plot of the *t*-distribution for samples of size N = 4 and N = 25.

sample mean of $\bar{X} = 21$ and a sample-estimated population standard deviation $\hat{\sigma} = 1.15$. From here, we proceed with our typical model comparison steps and first assume that $\mathcal{H}_0$ is true – that is, that $\mu = 23$. We convert our observed data to a standardized score – now called a *t*-score – as follows:

$$t = \frac{\bar{X} - \mu}{\hat{\sigma} / \sqrt{N}}$$

$$= \frac{21 - 23}{1.15 / \sqrt{4}}$$

$$= \frac{-2}{1.15 / 2}$$

$$= \frac{-2}{0.575}$$

$$= -3.48.$$

Remember that our goal is to test how surprising our data is *if the null is true*. For this, we compute the *p*-value, which is the probability of observing our data (or more extreme) under the null model. Thus, we need to find the probability of

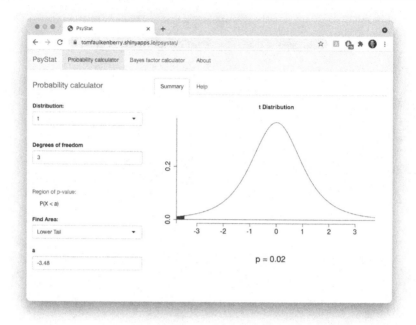

Figure 6.2 A screenshot of *PsyStat* showing a one-tailed test on a *t*-distribution.

getting a *t*-score less than or equal to −3.48; that is, $p = P(t \leq -3.48)$. To find this, we use our PsyStat app (see Figure 6.2). This time, under "Distribution:" we'll select the option "t". You'll notice immediately that the user input fields change a bit – since the *t*-distribution depends on sample size, there will be a field which lets us specify this.

Actually, I am misleading you a bit, but hear me out. The field is actually called "Degrees of freedom", which is equal to one less than the sample size (i.e., $N-1$). Simply put, **degrees of freedom** (or *df* for short) is the bias-corrected denominator that we used to compute the estimated value of the population standard deviation. For various reasons, it is much more common to specify a *t*-distribution with degrees of freedom than with sample size, so we adopt that convention here as well. For us, we have $N = 4$, so the degrees of freedom is one less; that is, $df = N-1 = 4-1 = 3$.

Finally, we need to specify the region for the *p*-value. Here, we want to know the probability of getting a *t*-score *less* than or equal to −3.48, so this time, we will choose "Lower Tail" in the "Find Area:" field. Then, we'll specify the observed *t*-score in the "a" field as −3.48. As you can see in Figure 6.2, the output automatically updates to show us that $p = 0.02$ (along with a small area shaded in the left tail).

So, what do we make of this *p*-value? Remember, we assumed that $\mathcal{H}_0 : \mu = 23$ was the correct model. If this is the case, then the probability of obtaining our actually observed data ($\overline{X} = 21$) is pretty small: $p = 0.02$. Since it is below the customary threshold of 0.05, we consider that these data are *rare* under the null, and as a result, we reject the null model $\mathcal{H}_0$ in favor of the alternative model $\mathcal{H}_1 : \mu < 23$. That is, I can conclude that the curriculum revisions that I made in my statistics courses result in significantly fewer errors compared to before.

Confidence intervals

In the previous section, we rejected the null model $\mathcal{H}_0 : \mu = 23$ in favor of the alternative model $\mathcal{H}_1 : \mu < 23$. From this, we conclude that μ, the population mean number of errors for all possible statistics courses that could potentially be taught under the revised curriculum, is indeed smaller than 23. From this we conclude that the revised curriculum works – students make, on average, fewer errors.

But how many fewer? Indeed, as I mentioned at the end of Chapter 5, the model comparison procedure alone does not give us any indication of the magnitude of the effect; only *that* the effect exists. To find out how many fewer errors are made under the revised curriculum, we will need to estimate the value of μ. In Chapter 5, we learned that this is done with a *confidence interval*.

Recall from Chapter 5 that we can estimate a 95% confidence interval for an unknown population mean μ by using the sample mean $\bar{X}$ and the population standard deviation σ as follows:

$$95\% \text{ Confidence interval} = \bar{X} \pm 1.96 \cdot \frac{\sigma}{\sqrt{N}}.$$

Immediately, we see the same issue as before – what do we do if we are not given the value of the population standard deviation σ? In the previous section, we learned that we can *estimate* σ by dividing by $N-1$ instead of N when computing the variance; that is,

$$\hat{\sigma} = \sqrt{\frac{SS}{N-1}}.$$

Can we use $\hat{\sigma}$ in the place of σ in the confidence interval formula above?

Well, essentially yes, but there is a catch. *We have to also adjust the 1.96 in the formula too.* Let's discuss why this is the case.

First, let's recall where the 1.96 comes from. In our development of the 95% confidence interval from Chapter 5, we used the Central Limit Theorem to reason that there was a 95% probability of any given sample mean falling roughly two standard deviations (really, standard errors) from the population mean μ. I always say "roughly two", but in reality, that number is exactly 1.96 – for a *normal distribution* anyway (see the leftmost pane of Figure 6.3). But for a *t*-distribution, things change. As we discovered earlier, the shape of the *t*-distribution changes with differing sample sizes. Specifically, the tails of the *t*-distribution get fatter as the sample size (and equivalently, degrees

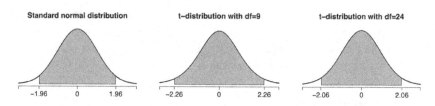

Figure 6.3 Three plots showing the critical values of the *t*-distribution under three different sample sizes.

of freedom) decrease. To see this, consider the center and right panes of the figure below. The center pane represents the *t*-distribution that arises from samples of size $N = 10$ (i.e., $df = 9$), whereas the rightmost pane represents the *t*-distribution for samples of size $N = 25$ ($df = 24$). Because the difference is slight, it is difficult to see from the figures alone that the tails are slightly fatter for the $df = 9$ curve than for the $df = 24$ curve. But this is confirmed by looking at the values displayed on the horizontal axes. For the rightmost curve ($df = 24$), 95% of *t*-scores fall between the values $t = -2.06$ and $t = 2.06$. For the center curve ($df = 9$), the range is even wider, with 95% of *t*-scores falling between $t = -2.26$ and $t = 2.26$.

What is the significance of these numbers? When constructing a 95% confidence interval, we need to know that **critical value** of the distribution which defines the limits of the range holding 95% of the possible sample means that would arise under the null model. So, if we are to have any hope of constructing a 95% confidence interval for situations where we have to estimate σ from our observed data, then we need to know these critical values for the *t*-distribution. From Figure 6.3, we can see that while the critical value for the standard normal distribution is always 1.96, the critical value for the *t*-distribution will be different for every possible sample size. Thus, to calculate our interval, we need a way to find these critical values.

In the past, textbooks would include tables of critical values for each possible value of df. Instead of using a table, I built our PsyStat app to automatically display the critical values for us! Here's how it works – when you select "t" from the "Distribution:" menu, you are then prompted to select the "Degrees of freedom". Go ahead and enter the degrees of freedom; for example, let's enter $df = 9$. If you'll then select "Both Tails" from the "Find Area:" menu, the display will automatically update to show you a *t*-distribution with two symmetric tails shaded to include almost exactly 5%. Furthermore, it will show you the endpoints of the left and right tails in the "a" and "b" text boxes – in this case, it automatically updates to -2.26 and 2.26, respectively. These are exactly the same values as displayed in the center pane of the figure above – they are the critical values of the *t*-distribution for $df = 9$. Similarly, when you change the degrees of freedom to 24, you will see that they automatically update to -2.06 and 2.06.

With this in mind, let's now consider a general method to construct 95% confidence intervals when we are not given the population standard deviation σ. In this situation, we will define the 95% confidence interval as

$$\bar{X} \pm t^{*}_{df} \cdot \frac{\hat{\sigma}}{\sqrt{N}},$$

where t^{*}_{df} is the positive critical value of the *t*-distribution with degrees of freedom equal to df. Hopefully you'll notice that this form is almost identical to our previous definition of the 95% confidence interval. The only difference is that instead of a critical value of 1.96, we will have a different critical value for different values of df.

Now we can work out a 95% confidence interval for the problem we began the chapter with. In our work above, we calculated a sample mean of $\bar{X} = 21$ and an estimated population standard deviation $\hat{\sigma} = 1.15$. Also, we recall our sample size is $N = 4$. The only thing that remains to be found before calculating the confidence interval is the critical value. In our PsyStat app (see Figure 6.4), we can find this by specifying degrees of freedom equal to $df = N - 1$. In this

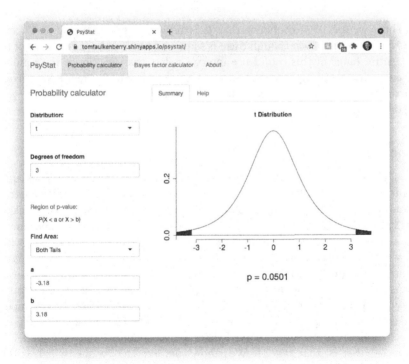

Figure 6.4 A screenshot of *PsyStat* showing the critical values for a *t*-distribution with $df = 3$.

case, that comes out to $df = 3$. As we can see in Figure 6.4, PsyStat updates its display to immediately give us the critical value as $t_3^* = 3.18$.

From these values, the computation of the confidence interval carries out as usual:

$$CI = \left(\bar{X} - t_3^* \cdot \frac{\hat{\sigma}}{\sqrt{N}}, \bar{X} + t_3^* \cdot \frac{\hat{\sigma}}{\sqrt{N}} \right)$$

$$= \left(21 - 3.18 \cdot \frac{1.15}{\sqrt{4}}, 21 + 3.18 \cdot \frac{1.15}{\sqrt{4}} \right)$$

$$= \left(21 - 3.18 \cdot \frac{1.15}{2}, 21 + 3.18 \cdot \frac{1.15}{2} \right)$$

$$= \left(21 - 3.18 \cdot 0.575, 21 + 3.18 \cdot 0.575 \right)$$

$$= \left(21 - 1.8285, 21 + 1.8285 \right)$$

$$= \left(19.1715, 22.8285 \right).$$

Thus, we are 95% confident that μ is between approximately 19.17 and 22.83. Notice that even though there is some uncertainty about the value of μ, the entire range of this confidence interval is less than 23. So, in the context of our original research question, our inference is that the revised statistics curriculum resulted in significantly fewer errors than were typically observed before the intervention.

Another example

Now equipped with all the techniques we need for the *t*-test and associated confidence intervals, let's walk through one more complete example. To save some time, I'll just present the summary statistics rather than the raw data. Let's suppose we have a sample of $N = 25$ people who is given an experimental treatment. After the treatment, we find a sample mean of $\bar{X} = 22.2$ with $SS = 384$. Let μ represent the population mean of the treatment group. Is μ significantly greater than 21?

As before, we'll employ our two complementary approaches to answering this question. First, let's perform a model comparison. We'll consider two models: a null model $\mathcal{H}_0 : \mu = 21$ and an alternative model $\mathcal{H}_1 : \mu > 21$. To compare these models against the observed data, we first assume the null model is correct – that is, that $\mu = 21$. We'll now compute the *p*-value, which is the probability of observing our data (or more extreme) under this null model.

Recall that to compute the *p*-value, we need to transform the sample mean $\bar{X}$ into a standardized score (i.e., a z-score or a *t*-score). Since we are not given the population standard deviation σ, we'll need to estimate it from the observed data, and then use this estimate to compute a *t*-score. To this end, we compute $\hat{\sigma}$ as:

$$\hat{\sigma} = \sqrt{\frac{SS}{N-1}}$$

$$= \sqrt{\frac{384}{25-1}}$$

$$= \sqrt{\frac{384}{24}}$$

$$= \sqrt{16}$$

$$= 4.$$

Given this value for $\hat{\sigma}$, we may now proceed with computing the *t*-score for our observed data:

$$t = \frac{\bar{X}-\mu}{\hat{\sigma}/\sqrt{N}}$$

$$= \frac{22.2-21}{4/\sqrt{25}}$$

$$= \frac{1.2}{4/5}$$

$$= \frac{1.2}{0.8}$$

$$= 1.5.$$

So, our observed data ($\bar{X} = 22.2$) gives us a *t*-score equal to 1.5. Now we ask how likely this data (or more extreme) would be if the null model were correct (i.e., the *p*-value). To do this, we use our PsyStat app – remember to set $df = 25-1 = 24$, select "Upper Tail", and set "a" equal to our observed *t*-score (1.5):

$$p = P(\bar{X} \geq 22.2)$$

$$= P(t \geq 1.5)$$

$$= 0.0733.$$

The *p*-value of 0.0733 means that there is a 7.33% chance of observing our data (or more extreme) if the null is correct. Since this does not fall below our customary threshold of 5%, we consider these data to be somewhat plausible under the null. Thus, we fail to reject the null, and as such, cannot conclude that μ is significantly greater than 21.

So how big is μ? All we know at this point is that it is not likely to be much greater than 21. To answer this, we can compute a 95% confidence interval for μ. Recall that the form for this confidence interval is given by

$$\bar{X} \pm t^*_{df} \cdot \frac{\hat{\sigma}}{\sqrt{N}}.$$

From our earlier work, we already know everything we need except for the critical value t^*_{24}. But it is an easy exercise to get it from our PsyStat app – simply reload the app in the browser and select 24 for the "Degrees of freedom" again. The display will automatically update to show a critical value of 2.06. Thus, we can compute

$$CI = \left(\bar{X} - t^*_{24} \cdot \frac{\hat{\sigma}}{\sqrt{N}}, \bar{X} + t^*_{24} \cdot \frac{\hat{\sigma}}{\sqrt{N}} \right)$$

$$= \left(22.2 - 2.06 \cdot \frac{4}{\sqrt{25}}, 22.2 + 2.06 \cdot \frac{4}{\sqrt{25}} \right)$$

$$= \left(22.2 - 2.06 \cdot \frac{4}{5}, 22.2 + 2.06 \cdot \frac{4}{5} \right)$$

$$= \left(22.2 - 2.06 \cdot 0.8, 22.2 + 2.06 \cdot 0.8 \right)$$

$$= \left(22.2 - 1.648, 22.2 + 1.648 \right)$$

$$= \left(20.552, 23.848 \right).$$

Thus, we are 95% confident that μ is between approximately 20.55 and 23.85.

The road ahead

There is much more to say about the *t*-test, but what you've learned so far is plenty to get a feel for how everything works. The key to remember is that the *t*-test arises from a very common situation – namely, those contexts in which we do not know the standard deviation of the population. Because this is so common in most experimental design contexts, the *t*-test is usually the correct test to perform when seeking to assess the efficacy of an experimental treatment.

One thing that I should mention in passing is there are multiple types of *t*-tests that can be performed, and I'll briefly mention them here. In practice, we usually use computer software packages (such as JASP or R) to compute the *p*-values and associated confidence intervals. But I can describe them conceptually here:

- The **paired-samples *t*-test** is used in the context where experimental units (i.e., participants in a study) are measured on two occasions. For example, a common context is in a **repeated measures design**, where people are given a pretest, administered an experimental treatment, and then given a posttest. We then might want to know whether scores increased from pretest to posttest. To do this, our sample would then consist of *difference scores* for each participant – that is, for each person, we compute the difference between their pretest score and their posttest score. These difference scores then form a single sample, from which we can compute the mean and standard deviation. This allows us to perform model comparison and estimation in exactly the same way we did throughout this chapter.
- The **independent samples *t*-test** is used when we want to compare the means of two *independent* (nonoverlapping) samples. This is a very common experimental context (sometimes called a "between subjects design"). For example, you might want to compare the test scores of two classes – one of which learned material using one method, and the other which learned material using another method. These two classes are *independent* in the sense that the students are in either one class or the other – not both. That is, the two classes do not overlap. The mathematical formulation of the independent samples *t*-test is quite a bit more complicated than what I described in this chapter, but the actions we perform are conceptually similar. In essence, we convert our observed data (this time, two sample means and two standard deviations) into a single *t*-score, from which we can compute a *p*-value.

As you go on in your statistical education, you'll notice that most statistical methods you encounter from here on will be formulated on similar conceptual grounds. The main idea is that we convert our observed data into some "test statistic", and then we compute a *p*-value from that test statistic. *The p-value is always a number which tells us the likelihood of our data (or more extreme) under the assumption that the null model is correct.* We use this number to tell us about the plausibility of the null hypothesis. If the plausibility is small (i.e., the data is rare under the null), this tells us to reject the null as a model of our population – in its place, we get some indirect support for the alternative. If the plausibility is not small (i.e., $p > 0.05$), we cannot reject the null.

In fact, not being able to reject the null leaves us in a bit of a predicament. We cannot reject the null, but we cannot "accept" it either. In other words, while we can obtain evidence (albeit indirect) *for* the alternative, we can never obtain any evidence *for* the null. The logic of our inferential procedure only allows us to rule out the null as a plausible model, but never to *retain* the null. To do that, we need a fundamentally different method of inference. That method, called *Bayesian inference* is the topic of the next chapter.

Chapter summary

In this chapter, we learned about the *t*-test. Here is a recap of the high points:

1 The *t*-test is used in situations where the population standard deviation is unknown.
2 Computing a *t*-score is exactly like computing a *z*-score, with one exception – since σ is unknown, we have to *estimate* its value.
3 The estimated standard deviation, denoted $\hat{\sigma}$ is computed as:

$$\hat{\sigma} = \sqrt{\frac{\sum (X_i - \bar{X})^2}{N-1}}.$$

4 Conceptually, the estimated standard deviation σ is computed just like the usual standard deviation, but instead of dividing the sum of squares by N, we divide by $N-1$. The reason is that standard deviations computed from samples tend to underestimate the true value of the population standard deviation σ. To compensate, we divide by a slightly smaller number (i.e., $N-1$).
5 The distribution of *t*-scores forms a distribution that looks normal, but it isn't – it has slightly "fatter" tails (i.e., more of the distribution is in the tail region than compared to the normal distribution). Further, the exact shape of the *t*-distribution depends on the sample size. We use a quantity called *degrees of freedom* (i.e., $df = N-1$) to describe the specific *t*-distribution we use.
6 Confidence intervals are computed similarly, but instead of using the number 1.96 to define the inner 95% of the distribution, we have to use the *critical value* of the *t*-distribution that arises in each specific example. These critical values are easily found in the PsyStat app.
7 Even though our examples were all *single sample t*-tests, the concepts can be extended to *paired samples* designs and *independent samples* designs.

Supplementary video lecture

If you would like to watch an online video lecture where I discuss the concepts we talked about in this chapter, you can navigate your web browser to https://youtu.be/hlISFDoOjmQ. Additionally, I have put together two more lectures where I specifically talk about the independent samples *t*-test. The first, where I cover the mechanics of the test itself, is at https://youtu.be/2fIldYR3is4. The second, where I discuss confidence intervals for *t*-test designs (including the independent samples *t*-test) is at https://youtu.be/s24rWU2T6H4.

Exercises

1 A random sample of $N = 16$ individuals is selected from a population with $\mu = 35$, and a treatment is administered to each individual in the sample. After treatment, the sample mean is found to be $\bar{X} = 37.4$ with $SS = 290$. Based on the sample data, does the treatment result in a significant increase?

2 To evaluate the effect of a treatment, a sample is obtained from a population with a mean of $\mu = 50$ and the treatment is administered to the individuals in the sample. After treatment, the sample mean is found to be 50.9 with a standard deviation of $\hat{\sigma} = 4$.

    a   If the sample consists of $N = 25$ individuals, are the data sufficient to conclude that the treatment results in a significant increase?

    b   If the sample consists of $N = 64$ individuals, are the data sufficient to conclude that the treatment results in a significant increase?

    c   Comparing your answers for parts (a) and (b), how does the size of the sample influence the outcome of a hypothesis test?

3 Research using various standardized measures of anxiety indicate that anxiety levels have increased over the past half century (Twenge, 2000). For example, in the 1950s the average score on the Child Manifest Anxiety Scale was $\mu = 15.1$. A sample of $N = 16$ of today's children produces a mean score of $\bar{X} = 17.7$ with $SS = 225$. Based on this sample, has there been a significant change in the average level of anxiety since the 1950s?

4 A researcher surveys a group of university students to determine level of life satisfaction among first year students. For a sample of 36 students, the average observed life satisfaction score was 14.5, with $SS = 183.2$. Construct a 95% confidence interval for the population mean life satisfaction score among first year university students.

Chapter 7

Bayesian model comparison

Ah, Bayesian statistics. If you've been lurking around in the behavioral sciences for the past decade, you've undoubtedly heard people talking about Bayesian statistics. Many times, these conversations span quite a range of emotional valence, from quiet admiration to outright claims of witchcraft. Despite its recent surge in popularity, Bayesian methods of inference are still relatively "cutting edge". Relatedly, there are not many accessible gateways to learning about Bayesian statistics, though I'll certainly admit there are far more resources available now compared to when I was learning it myself over a decade ago. My goal in this chapter is to introduce you to a small component of Bayesian statistics that will be very useful to overcome some of the issues I've foreshadowed in previous chapters. Specifically, we will learn about **Bayesian model comparison**.

As always, I will motivate our discussion by presenting an example. Suppose we are interested in assessing the effectiveness of a peer-review program in teaching undergraduate psychology majors to write effectively. To assess our undergraduates' writing ability in psychology, we use the Scale for Assessing Writing in Psychology. This scale, which we'll abbreviate as the SAW-P, is a nationally normed assessment with a known population mean score of 50.

After implementing our peer-review program for a semester, we administer the SAW-P to our undergraduates and find that our sample of $N = 65$ students had a mean score of $\overline{X} = 54.4$ and a standard deviation of $\hat{\sigma} = 10$. Given these data, can we conclude that our peer-review program worked? That is, did it increase the scores of our undergraduates on the SAW-P compared to the national average?

At this point in the book, you've seen similar scenarios many times. You have already learned that one way to answer this question is to define two competing models – a null model $\mathcal{H}_0$ where the training did not work, and an alternative model $\mathcal{H}_1$ where the training *did* work. Then, we perform a model comparison, assessing the fit of these models against the observed data. In both Chapters 5 and 6, we used the p-value to perform the model comparison. Recall that the p-value is the likelihood of observing our data (or more

DOI: 10.4324/9781003181828-7

extreme) *if the null model is correct.* If the p-value is small (i.e., $p < 0.05$), we see that our observed data would be rare under the null hypothesis. Considering that we've already observed this supposedly rare data, we reason that the null model must not be correct, thus rejecting it in favor of the alternative.

Two issues arise immediately with this procedure. First, our evidence for the alternative model $\mathcal{H}_1$ is only *indirect*. By observing a small p-value, we've shown the observed data are very unlikely if the null is true. Given that we've already observed these data, this tells us that the null is not a good fit for our observed data. *But nowhere have we actually assessed how well the alternative model $\mathcal{H}_1$ fits our data.* The game of model comparison with the p-value plays out like a forfeited tennis match. Sure, if we reject the null model $\mathcal{H}_0$ on the basis of a small p-value, the alternative model $\mathcal{H}_1$ "wins", but how do we know it is even a reasonable model itself?

A second issue reveals the opposite problem. What happens when we fail to reject the null model $\mathcal{H}_0$ because we observe a p-value *greater* than 0.05? By definition, this means that the data are at least somewhat plausible under the null model, so maybe it is still a good fit for the data. But again, this p-value does not provide any measure of evidence *for* $\mathcal{H}_0$. Mathematically, it can be shown that the distribution of all possible p-values that could arise from data generated under a null model is a *uniform* distribution. That is, a p-value of 0.1 is just as likely to occur as a p-value of 0.9. If we wanted to use the p-value to provide a measure of evidence for the null, then $p = 0.9$ should represent a greater amount of evidence than $p = 0.1$. But it doesn't. Because both p-values are equally likely under the null, $p = 0.9$ doesn't tell us anything different from $p = 0.1$, except that we *cannot reject* the null.

The Bayes factor

To overcome these problems, we need a different method for performing our model comparison. In Bayesian model comparison, we use a different tool for inference called the **Bayes factor** (Jeffreys, 1961; Kass & Raftery, 1995). Mathematically, the Bayes factor can be written as a ratio

$$\mathrm{BF}_{10} = \frac{P(\text{data} \mid \mathcal{H}_1)}{P(\text{data} \mid \mathcal{H}_0)}.$$

This fraction allows us to simultaneously assess the likelihood of the observed data under both $\mathcal{H}_1$ and $\mathcal{H}_0$. For example, suppose $\mathrm{BF}_{10} = 4$. This Bayes factor tells us that the numerator $P(\text{data} \mid \mathcal{H}_1)$ is 4 times larger than the denominator $P(\text{data} \mid \mathcal{H}_0)$. Thus, we can say that the observed data are 4 times more likely under $\mathcal{H}_1$ than under $\mathcal{H}_0$. This overcomes the first issue above – here, we have *direct* evidence for $\mathcal{H}_1$. Rather than simply rejecting the null model $\mathcal{H}_0$, we can quantify the extent to which the alternative model $\mathcal{H}_1$ is a better predictor of the data.

We can go further. What if we had $BF_{10} = 1/4$? In this case, the Bayes factor tells us that the numerator $P(\text{data} \mid \mathcal{H}_1)$ is 4 times *smaller* than the denominator $P(\text{data} \mid \mathcal{H}_0)$. Said differently, the observed data are 4 times more likely under the null model $\mathcal{H}_0$ than under the alternative model $\mathcal{H}_1$. In this instance, we can interpret this as direct evidence for $\mathcal{H}_0$, something which is impossible to do with p-values.

The fact that the Bayes factor can directly index support for *either* the null model $\mathcal{H}_0$ or the alternative model $\mathcal{H}_1$ is a major advantage. Because of this, we must be careful when reporting Bayes factors to clearly indicate the model which is being supported. With p-values, no such care is needed, because the p-value *always* represents the fit of the data against the null. For Bayes factors, we specify the model being supported by the notation of the subscript. There are two ways to write any given Bayes factor – either as the likelihood of the data under the alternative compared to the null:

$$ BF_{10} = \frac{P(\text{data} \mid \mathcal{H}_1)}{P(\text{data} \mid \mathcal{H}_0)}, $$

or we can write it as the likelihood of the data under the null compared to the alternative:

$$ BF_{01} = \frac{P(\text{data} \mid \mathcal{H}_0)}{P(\text{data} \mid \mathcal{H}_1)}. $$

Note the difference in the subscripts. In the first one, the subscript is 10; this is not a number, but rather a specification of the direction of comparison. Thus it is read "one-zero", not "ten". In the second, the subscript is 01 (read "zero-one"). Note that these two expressions are reciprocals of each other – that is, $BF_{01} = 1/BF_{10}$. This is easily verified for our example above, as the reciprocal of $BF_{10} = 4$ is $BF_{01} = 1/4$ (the other direction holds as well, as $1/(1/4) = 4$).

One might think that all this flexibility in notation could result in some ambiguity, but in reality there is no such problem. Which do we report: BF_{01} or BF_{10}? For any given data, one of these will always be greater than 1 and the other less than 1. I generally recommend always reporting Bayes factors as a number greater than 1. I have found that it is generally easier to interpret this way. For example, in our example above, I would report $BF_{01} = 4$ rather than $BF_{10} = 1/4$. They're both mathematically telling us the same thing, but I find that the former is easier to understand.

Computing Bayes factors

I fear that what I am about to show you might give you the wrong impression. In general, computing Bayes factors is really hard (see the next section for some indication about why this is the case). Thankfully, many tools have been developed in the last decade to help with computing Bayes factors, and we will put those to use here. In fact, those tools are already built into our PsyStat app. In this section, we will work through our leading example and describe how to use PsyStat to compute a Bayes factor.

In our example about measuring psychology students' writing abilities (described above), we observed a mean score of $\bar{X} = 54.4$ and a standard deviation of $\hat{\sigma} = 10$ in a sample of $N = 65$ students. We want to know whether these scores represent an increase over the general population mean score of 50.

The first step is to define our competing models. As before, we define a null model $\mathcal{H}_0$, where the training did not work, and an alternative model, $\mathcal{H}_1$, where the training did work. When computing Bayes factors there is a slight difference in how these models are defined. Whereas our models before were defined in terms of the population mean μ, these models will involve both the population mean μ and the population standard deviation σ. The way we do this is in terms of **effect size**, which in this context is defined as

$$\delta = \frac{\mu - 50}{\sigma}.$$

The Greek letter δ (pronounced "delta") represents the size of the "effect" of our peer-review program in writing (i.e., the difference between our population's mean and the general population mean of 50). This difference is then scaled (or divided) by the standard deviation of our population, σ. There are some technical reasons for defining the models this way in terms of effect size (see Rouder et al., 2009), but doing so translates our models as follows:

- $\mathcal{H}_0 : \delta = 0$ (i.e., the effect size is 0), and
- $\mathcal{H}_1 : \delta > 0$ (i.e., the effect size is greater than 0).

Clearly, if our peer-review program worked, then we should see more support for $\mathcal{H}_1$ than for $\mathcal{H}_0$. How much more support do we see (if any)? Let's perform a Bayesian model comparison and compute BF_{10}, the Bayes factor for $\mathcal{H}_1$ over $\mathcal{H}_0$.

In PsyStat (go to https://tomfaulkenberry.shinyapps.io/psystat), you'll choose the tab labeled "Bayes factor calculator". This will then display to us several options. The first of these is whether the Bayes factor will be computed from a t-test or something called an ANOVA. ANOVA (i.e., analysis of variance) is beyond the scope of this book (see Chapter 8 for a brief description), but examples of how this calculator can be used with ANOVA can be found in Faulkenberry (2019). In our example, we have a single sample t-test, so we will select "t-test" under the "Test:" menu and "Single sample" under the "Design:" menu. Finally, we need to select our "Predicted direction:" – since we are hypothesizing that the scores will *increase*, we are predicting a "Positive effect", so we should select that option. Note that for now, I will ignore the "Prior probability of null:" field; I'll describe that in the next section.

From here, we can see that there are numeric input fields for the "t-statistic:" and the "Sample size:". We already know the sample size is $N = 65$, so we can enter 65 in the sample size field. All that is left is the t-statistic, which we can compute readily from the information we have been given:

$$
\begin{aligned}
t &= \frac{\bar{X} - \mu}{\hat{\sigma}/\sqrt{N}} \\
&= \frac{54.4 - 50}{10/\sqrt{65}} \\
&= \frac{4.4}{10/8.06} \\
&= \frac{4.4}{1.24} \\
&= 3.55.
\end{aligned}
$$

Thus, we can put 3.55 into the "t-statistic:" field. The output of the app will immediately update to reflect the results of our model comparison (see Figure 7.1). Let's go through this output. At the top of the output, we are given a reminder of how the two competing models $\mathcal{H}_0$ and $\mathcal{H}_1$ are defined. Next, we see a pie chart (also called a "pizza plot") that visually depicts the predictive adequacy of our two competing models. The purple slice represents the relative likelihood of observing the data under $\mathcal{H}_0$, whereas the white slice represents the relative likelihood of observing the data under $\mathcal{H}_1$. We can see that the white slice is *much* larger than the purple slice – we interpret this to mean that the data are much more likely under $\mathcal{H}_1$ than under $\mathcal{H}_0$. How much more? This question is answered in the next part of the output – it is the Bayes factor. From these data, we get a Bayes factor of $\mathrm{BF}_{10} = 69.37$, along with an explanation that this means that the observed data are approximately 69.37 times more likely under $\mathcal{H}_1$ than under $\mathcal{H}_0$.

So, we can see that our data support a model where the peer-review program has a *positive* effect on the writing scores. Notice that this support is not indirect, which is what we get when we the traditional "reject the null" procedure described in earlier chapters. Here, the Bayes factor simultaneously assesses the predictive adequacy of *both* models and tells us succinctly that the data are much more likely under the positive effect model $\mathcal{H}_1$ than under the null model $\mathcal{H}_0$. And moreover, this information was easy to obtain – all we needed to do was feed a t-score into our PsyStat app.

At this point, you might be wondering if there is a threshold for Bayes factors (like $p = 0.05$ for p-values). The answer is "it's complicated". In general, many Bayesians (including myself) argue that Bayes factors should be interpreted

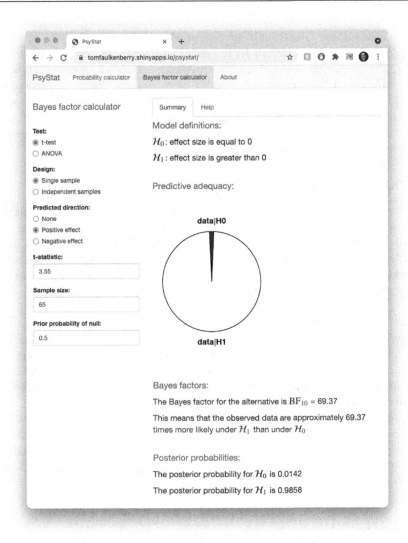

Figure 7.1 A screenshot of the *PsyStat* "Bayes Factor Calculator" module.

as continuous measures of evidence for a specific model over another, not in a thresholded "support/reject" dichotomy. Certainly, the bigger the Bayes factor, the greater the evidence. What then might be the smallest Bayes factor that could be considered as evidential for either $\mathcal{H}_1$ or $\mathcal{H}_0$? Generally, this minimum is recommended to be 3. One intuitive reason for this can be seen via the following exercise. In the same PsyStat window as before (i.e., with the settings we applied for the previous problem), see what happens when you change the *t*-score to 2.29. In this case, you'll see that the Bayes factor is just a little bigger than 3, meaning that the data are 3 times more likely under $\mathcal{H}_1$ than under $\mathcal{H}_0$. In this case, these "3-to-1 odds" mean that 75% of the pizza plot is in favor of $\mathcal{H}_1$. Any Bayes factor less than 3 will result in a smaller fraction in favor of $\mathcal{H}_1$. But what is special about this 75% threshold? Absolutely nothing! In fact, anything over a Bayes factor of 1 would cover more than 50% of the pizza plot, and thus would "support" $\mathcal{H}_1$, but most consider this as "anecdotal" support until it reaches the 75% point. This discussion could go on for days. Let's just end with noting that Bayes factors, whatever their value, should be interpreted fully, not just listed as a magical number with no context.

What is "Bayesian" about Bayes factors?

In this section, I want to provide some more technical background on Bayes factors. This section can be safely skipped, but the main aim here is that we will develop another interpretation of the Bayes factor; this time as an *updating factor*. This interpretation allows us to use the Bayes factor to compute the **posterior probability** of each of our competing models; that is, the probability of each model *after* observing data.

At its root, Bayesian model comparison is possible because of something called **Bayes' Theorem** (or Bayes' Rule; see McGrayne, 2012), named after Reverend Thomas Bayes, an 18th century English minister and statistician who worked out how to compute probabilities in so-called "inverse problems". Recall that in our earlier chapters, we defined the p-value as the probability of observing some data, given that the null model is correct. Inverse problems switch this conditional statement, so a natural inverse problem to solve in this context would be to work out the probability that the null model is true, given the observed data. We can write this loosely in symbols. Whereas the p-value gives us something like $P(\text{data} \mid \mathcal{H}_0)$, we might be more interested in $P(\mathcal{H}_0 \mid \text{data})$. Bayes theorem says that we can compute this so-called *posterior probability* as follows:

$$P(\mathcal{H}_0 \mid \text{data}) = \underbrace{P(\mathcal{H}_0)}_{\substack{\text{Prior beliefs} \\ \text{about } \mathcal{H}_0}} \times \underbrace{\frac{P(\text{data} \mid \mathcal{H}_0)}{P(\text{data})}}_{\text{predictive updating factor}} \; .$$

$\underbrace{}_{\substack{\text{Posterior beliefs} \\ \text{about } \mathcal{H}_0}}$

The under-brackets I've put on this equation help to interpret what each part means. The essence of Bayes' theorem is that our posterior belief about a specific model (e.g., $\mathcal{H}_0$) can be found by starting with our *prior* belief about the model, then multiplying this by a predictive updating factor. In this context, *posterior* simply means "after observing data", and *prior* means "before observing data". Thus, Bayes' theorem is really just a mathematical form of the scientific method – that is, we have a certain level of belief in something before seeing data, and that level of belief is updated after observing data. If the data is in line with the model, our posterior belief increases. On the other hand, if the data is not in line with the model, our posterior belief decreases.

For situations involving model comparison, Bayes' theorem becomes very useful when we simultaneously apply it to two models $\mathcal{H}_0$ and $\mathcal{H}_1$. If we consider the *posterior odds* of $\mathcal{H}_1$ and $\mathcal{H}_0$ (i.e., the ratio of the two posterior probabilities), we can use Bayes' theorem to see that there is a similar updating process from prior odds to posterior odds:

$$\underbrace{\frac{P(\mathcal{H}_1 \mid \text{data})}{P(\mathcal{H}_0 \mid \text{data})}}_{\substack{\text{posterior odds} \\ \text{of models}}} = \underbrace{\frac{P(\mathcal{H}_1)}{P(\mathcal{H}_0)}}_{\substack{\text{prior odds} \\ \text{of models}}} \times \underbrace{\frac{P(\text{data} \mid \mathcal{H}_1)}{P(\text{data} \mid \mathcal{H}_0)}}_{\text{predictive updating factor}} .$$

The predictive updating factor should look familiar:

$$\text{BF}_{10} = \frac{P(\text{data} \mid \mathcal{H}_1)}{P(\text{data} \mid \mathcal{H}_0)}$$

is the *Bayes factor*, and as we can see in the equation, it represents the factor by which our relative belief in $\mathcal{H}_1$ over $\mathcal{H}_0$ can be updated after observing data. This is a different interpretation of the Bayes factor from before, which only considered the relative predictive adequacy of the two models. One consequence of this "updating factor" interpretation is that we can use it to compute the posterior probability of the two models.

Briefly, here's how it works. Let's consider our two models $\mathcal{H}_0$ and $\mathcal{H}_1$ from the example above. To compute the posterior odds, we need to define the prior odds of the model. This is up to us. Each person can potentially define the prior odds differently, but one common default is to use *uniform* (or one-to-one) odds. That is, we assume that $P(\mathcal{H}_0)$ and $P(\mathcal{H}_1)$ are equal, and thus both equal to 0.50. One way to say this is that $\mathcal{H}_0$ and $\mathcal{H}_1$ are equally likely to be true *a priori*. Now, by the equation above, the posterior odds is equal to the prior odds multiplied by the Bayes factor. In our example, we got a Bayes factor of $\text{BF}_{10} = 69.37$. Thus, the posterior odds are equal to:

$$\begin{aligned}\frac{P(\mathcal{H}_1 \mid \text{data})}{P(\mathcal{H}_0 \mid \text{data})} &= \frac{P(\mathcal{H}_1)}{P(\mathcal{H}_0)} \times \frac{P(\text{data} \mid \mathcal{H}_1)}{P(\text{data} \mid \mathcal{H}_0)} \\ &= \frac{0.50}{0.50} \times BF_{10} \\ &= 1 \times 69.37 \\ &= 69.37.\end{aligned}$$

In other words, the posterior odds in favor of $\mathcal{H}_1$ are 69.37-to-1 over $\mathcal{H}_0$. From here, we can convert these posterior odds to posterior *probabilities*:

$$P\left(\mathcal{H}_1 \mid \text{data}\right) = \frac{69.37}{69.37 + 1}$$
$$= \frac{69.37}{70.37}$$
$$= 0.9858,$$

and

$$P\left(\mathcal{H}_0 \mid \text{data}\right) = \frac{1}{69.37 + 1}$$
$$= \frac{1}{70.37}$$
$$= 0.0142.$$

Notice that these posterior probabilities exactly match those given to us at the bottom of the PsyStat output in Figure 7.1. In fact, even if we have different prior odds that we would like to give each of our models, we can accommodate this in PsyStat by simply adjusting the "Prior probability of null:" field. Doing this will automatically adjust the resulting posterior probabilities. These adjustments are beyond the scope of this book, but the interested reader is invited to play around with them. Ultimately, regardless of your prior beliefs, the data speak very loudly, as they update these prior odds by a factor of almost 70! This means that even someone who is reasonably convinced that there is no effect *a priori* will have to multiply these odds by 69.37, pushing the posterior belief to a much higher value.

Bayesian re-analyses of previous examples

To give us more practice with computing and reporting Bayes factors, we will conclude this chapter by conducting Bayesian re-analyses of our previous examples in the past few chapters. Doing Bayesian re-analyses of published data is becoming more and more popular in the psychological sciences, and doing so is easy with tools like our PsyStat calculator (as well as free software-based tools like JASP). The interested reader should consult Ly et al. (2018) and Faulkenberry (2019) for a demonstration of these methods.

Here, we will perform re-analyses of the examples from Chapter 6. In the first example, we saw a sample of $N = 4$ statistics classes who on average made fewer errors on a standardized test. In that example, we found a t-score of -3.48 with $p = 0.02$. We interpreted this p-value as indicating that the observed data were rare if the null model were correct, thus concluding in favor of the alternative model. Recall that this "support" for $\mathcal{H}_1$ is indirect – with a Bayesian re-analysis, we can directly assess the evidence for each model.

Figure 7.2 shows such a re-analysis in PsyStat. As before, we choose the Test and Design to be a t-test and a single-sample design. For Predicted direction, we choose "Negative effect", as the alternative model predicts that the error

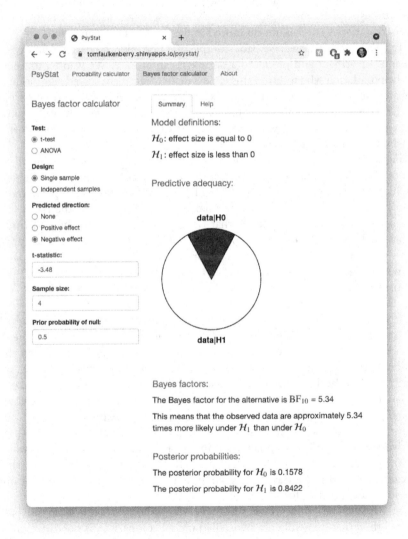

Figure 7.2 Screenshot of *PsyStat* displaying a Bayesian re-analysis of a *t*-test.

scores will *decrease*. Then we input our observed *t*-score (−3.48) and our sample size (4). We can see immediately in the output that the data are quite a bit more likely under the alternative model $\mathcal{H}_1$ than under the null model $\mathcal{H}_0$. The Bayes factor is $\mathrm{BF}_{10} = 5.34$, which we can interpret in two different ways. First, it means that the observed data are approximately 5.34 times more likely under $\mathcal{H}_1$ than under $\mathcal{H}_0$. Second, it means that our posterior odds in favor of $\mathcal{H}_1$ have been increased. If we assume equal prior odds, our relative belief in $\mathcal{H}_1$ has been increased by a factor of 5.34. This equates to posterior probabilities of $P(\mathcal{H}_1 \mid \mathrm{data}) = 0.8422$ and $P(\mathcal{H}_0 \mid \mathrm{data}) = 0.1578$. Thus, we have a reasonable amount of support for $\mathcal{H}_1$, indicating that the students who learned from the revised statistics curriculum do indeed make fewer errors than before.

In the second example, we had a sample of 25 people who received an experimental treatment and produced a sample mean of 22.2. We wanted to know if the population who received this experimental treatment scored significantly greater than 21. When we did this example in Chapter 6, we found a *t*-score of 1.5 with a *p*-value of 0.0733. Since we were not able to reject the null model $\mathcal{H}_0$ on the basis of this *p*-value, we were left quite inconclusive. What does a Bayesian re-analysis tell us?

Figure 7.3 shows us that the answer is, unfortunately, "not much". After we input the relevant summary statistics, we can see that the data are just about as likely under $\mathcal{H}_0$ as under $\mathcal{H}_1$. Though the data are ever so slightly more likely under $\mathcal{H}_1$, it is only by a very small amount. Specifically, the Bayes factor is $\mathrm{BF}_{10} = 1.04$, which tells us that the data are approximately 1.04 times more likely under $\mathcal{H}_1$ than under $\mathcal{H}_0$. If we assume equal prior odds, our prior odds have only been increased by a factor of 1.04 (i.e., only 4%). This equates to posterior probabilities of $P(\mathcal{H}_1 \mid \mathrm{data}) = 0.5098$ and $P(\mathcal{H}_0 \mid \mathrm{data}) = 0.4902$. Thus, these data provide very little evidential value to us, as they do not "tip the scales" toward either model.

It would be a shame to end here with such nonevidential data, so let's pull in one more example from Chapter 5. Even though we used *z*-scores there, the only difference between *z* and *t* is that *z* scores assume we are given the value of the population standard deviation. Thus, if we have a *z*-score, we can treat it exactly the same as a *t*-score in our PsyStat app. So, let's consider the last example of Chapter 5, where we observed game players' fluid intelligence scores. Our sample of 64 players had a mean score of 102 – we wanted to know whether this was significantly different from 100. Using a two-tailed model comparison, we found a *z*-score of 1.07 and a *p*-value of 0.285. Again, we cannot reject the null model $\mathcal{H}_0$ on the basis of this *p*-value, so we'll use a Bayesian re-analysis to determine to what extent are these data evidential for $\mathcal{H}_0$.

In PsyStat, we input these summary statistics as a *t*-test with no predicted direction (remember, a two-tailed model comparison is nondirectional. Figure 7.4 shows that we have some evidence in favor of the null model. The Bayes factor is $\mathrm{BF}_{01} = 4.23$, which again we can interpret in two different ways.

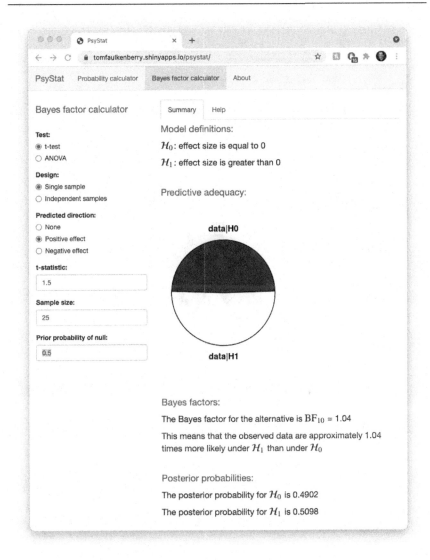

Figure 7.3 Screenshot of *PsyStat* showing data which is nonevidential for either model.

First, it means that the observed data are approximately 4.23 times more likely under $\mathcal{H}_0$ than under $\mathcal{H}_1$. Second, it means that our posterior odds in favor of $\mathcal{H}_0$ have been increased. If we assume equal prior odds, our relative belief in $\mathcal{H}_0$ has been increased by a factor of 4.23. This equates to posterior probabilities of $P\left(\mathcal{H}_0 \mid \text{data}\right) = 0.8089$ and $P\left(\mathcal{H}_0 \mid \text{data}\right) = 0.1911$. Thus, we have a reasonable amount of support for $\mathcal{H}_0$, indicating that players of this specific game have no different level of fluid intelligence compared to the general public.

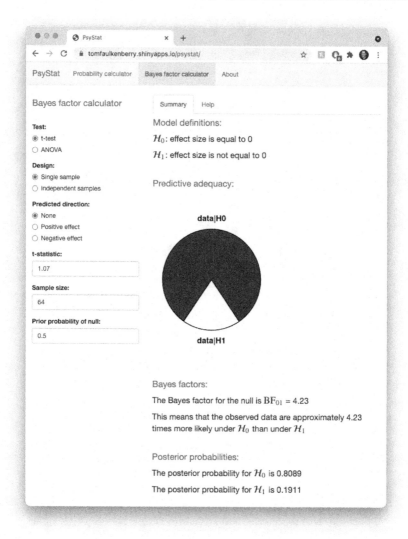

Figure 7.4 A screenshot from *PsyStat* showing data which is evidential for the null model.

Conclusion

There is so much more to say about Bayesian model comparison (and Bayesian statistics in general), but that's where I'll leave it for this book. In the next (and final) chapter, I'll wrap everything up by giving you a taste of "what's next", along with some specific recommendations for further reading. You now know everything you need to know to get started *doing* psychological statistics. From here, the sky is the limit. Regardless of the specific technique you might be applying or the type of software you might be using, the interpretations are always the same. A p-value is always a p-value in the sense you learned here – that is, the probability of observing some data (or more extreme) under the null model. A Bayes factor is always a Bayes factor in the sense you learned here – that is, the relative predictive adequacy of one model compared to another. If you keep these basic definitions in mind, you'll easily learn more and more advanced techniques for data analysis and you'll always be able to interpret the basic outputs of any statistical software package. Hopefully, if you ever get lost in the "weeds" of some advanced statistics down the road, you can come back to this book and quickly remind yourself of this basic knowledge. After all, my aim with this book was to provide you with "The Basics" of psychological statistics. I hope you enjoyed learning about it!

Supplementary video lecture

If you would like to watch an online video lecture where I discuss the concepts we talked about in this chapter, you can navigate your web browser to https://youtu.be/gnqDx8Zp8tk.

Exercises

For each of the problems below, you should do the following: (1) calculate and report the observed t-score; (2) calculate and report the resulting Bayes factor; and (3) calculate and report the posterior probability of the "winning" model (i.e., the model which receives more support from the data).

1   A random sample of $N = 35$ individuals is selected from a population with a mean of 60, and a treatment is administered to each individual in the sample. After treatment, the sample mean is found to be $\bar{X} = 60.2$ with $SS = 296$. Based on the sample data, can we conclude that the treatment results in a meaningful score change?

2   To evaluate the effect of a treatment, a sample of size 25 is obtained from a population with a mean of 20 and the treatment is administered to the individuals in the sample. After treatment, the sample mean is found to be $\bar{X} = 17.7$ with a standard deviation of $\hat{\sigma} = 3$. Is there a meaningful decrease that results from the treatment?

3   A sample of $N = 9$ individuals participates in a repeated measures study that produces a sample mean difference of $\bar{X} = 1.8$ with $SS = 135$ for the difference scores. Is this mean difference large enough to be considered a real effect? (*Hint: in a repeated measures study, a null effect would be a mean difference of 0*).

4   (a re-analysis of problem #3 from Chapter 6 exercises) In the 1950s, the average score on the Child Manifest Anxiety Scale was $\mu = 15.1$. A sample of $N = 16$ of today's children produces a mean score of $\bar{X} = 17.7$ with $SS = 225$. Based on this sample, has there been a significant change in the average level of anxiety since the 1950s?

Chapter 8

Recap and next steps

In the first seven chapters of this book, we have walked through the basics of psychological statistics. You have learned the conceptual underpinnings of two different types of statistical inference – one based on rejecting a null hypothesis with the p-value, and another based on assessing the relative evidence for two competing models with the Bayes factor. You have also learned some mechanics of how the most basic statistics are computed, from descriptive statistics such as the mean and standard deviation to inferential statistics like the t-score. It took seven chapters to do this because we had to learn a lot of new things along the way. In this concluding chapter, one of my aims is to tell the story of the first seven chapters all at once. If the previous chapters were akin to finding your way through a dark room, this final chapter should feel like turning on the light, thus letting you see where you were all along.

In Chapter 1, I used the Kanizsa (1976) triangle illusion to illustrate the framework of doing statistics in psychology and the behavioral sciences (see Figure 8.1). Recall that in this figure, an illusory triangle "pops out" of the middle between the three Pac-Man shaped anchors of (1) describing our data, (2) defining models, and (3) comparing the models. Much like the triangle, our game is one of *inference* – we use the things we *can* tangibly see and do (the three anchors) to "see" the things that we cannot.

So, let's turn on the light and see where we've been. As the goal of statistics in psychology is to answer research questions, let's start there and suppose we have a question for which we have designed an experiment and collected some data.

Let's begin at the top anchor: "Describing observed data". Here, our goal is to describe the data we've observed, usually in terms of center (e.g., mean) and variability (e.g., standard deviation). As we learned in Chapter 1, the mean is the average value, and the standard deviation is roughly the average amount that each observation differs from this mean.

Now that we've described the observed data, we want to perform inference in order to answer our research question. The next step is represented in the bottom right anchor: "Defining statistical models". The types of models (and how many) depend on the nature of the research questions, but for the common types of questions most often encountered in the psychological sciences,

DOI: 10.4324/9781003181828-8

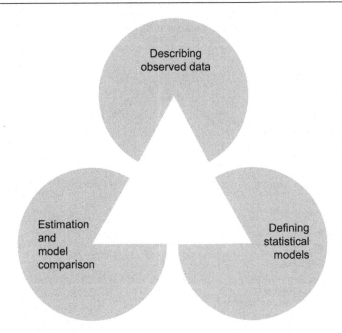

Figure 8.1 A framework for doing psychological statistics.

we usually consider two models on the unobservable population mean: (1) a null model $\mathcal{H}_0$, which states that there is no difference due to the experimental manipulation, and (2) an alternative model $\mathcal{H}_1$, which states that there *is* a difference. The nature of this difference under the alternative can be *directional*, which specifically states that there is an increase or decrease, or *nondirectional*, which simply states that there is a change (it may be either an increase or a decrease).

Once we've defined our competing models, we're ready to move the third anchor at the bottom left: "Estimation and model comparison". Here, we use the tools we developed throughout the book to estimate the value of the unobservable population mean with a confidence interval. Further, we can compare the two models in one of two ways. The classical way to do this model comparison involves computing the p-value, where we assume that the null model $\mathcal{H}_0$ is correct and compute the probability of observing our data (or more extreme) under the null. If this p-value is small (usually less than 0.05), that means that our observed data is rare under the null. But given that we've actually observed this data, the inference is that the null model must be incorrect. Thus, we reject it in favor of the alternative model $\mathcal{H}_1$. On the other hand, if the p-value is not small (i.e., greater than 0.05), we fail to reject the null – unfortunately, this does not let us conclude that the null is correct. Another way to perform this model comparison is to compute the Bayes factor, which indexes the

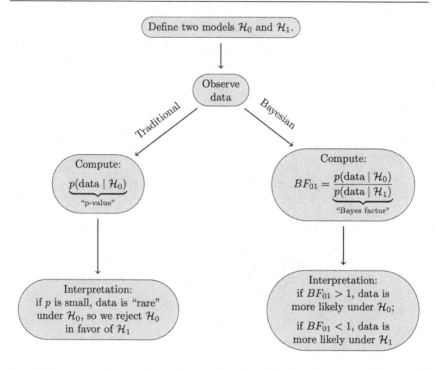

Figure 8.2 A diagram comparing the traditional and Bayesian approaches to model comparison.

relative likelihood of the observed data under each of the two models. The Bayes factor can be used to provide evidence for either the null model or the alternative model.

Before moving on to the next steps in your statistical journey, let's consider Figure 8.2. This figure gives us a concise diagram of the two statistical paths we've described. Starting at the top, we define two competing models of reality, and then we observe some data in order to test these models. The "traditional" path involves computing the p-value, and if this p-value is small, we reject the null model. The "Bayesian" path involves instead computing the Bayes factor, from which we get evidence for either the null or alternative. I hope this diagram will serve as a nice summary of the things you've learned throughout the book.

Next steps

One advantage to framing statistical inference via the figure above is that it nicely encapsulates most of the work we do in psychological statistics. So why is it that most statistics textbooks are hundreds of pages longer than this one? Partially, this is because traditional statistics textbooks cover many more types of research designs than I did in this book. To keep my focus on the *concepts* of psychological statistics, I specifically chose to focus only on one test – the *t*-test. It works well for research questions that involve at most two groups. But what about different types of research questions?

In this section, I will briefly outline some of the common designs (i.e., statistical tests) that you may encounter in your further study of psychological statistics. In most cases, the way in which these tests differ is in the definition of the models. Model comparison can still be done in terms of the *p*-value and the Bayes factor.

Analysis of variance

Analysis of variance (or **ANOVA** for short) was developed by Sir Ronald Fisher (1925) as a generalization of the *t*-test procedure that works for comparing *multiple* population means. Since then, the analysis of variance has become one of the most popular methods of model comparison in the experimental sciences. In its simplest form, the analysis of variance is designed to test for differences among multiple group means, making it useful for a wide variety of scientific investigations. In fact, its use is so ubiquitous in the psychological and behavioral sciences that Rouder et al. (2016) referred to the analysis of variance as the "workhorse" of experimental psychology.

The way that analysis of variance works is fundamentally different from the *t*-test. Recall that the *t*-test provides a measure of how far the sample mean is from a specific population mean via the *t*-score. When there are three or more groups, there is no longer a way to measure a single difference between means. To overcome this, analysis of variance works by partitioning the total *variance* in a set of observed data into two sources: the variance between experimental treatment groups, and the residual (i.e., left over) variance. Then, we calculate an *F*-statistic, which is defined as the ratio of the between-groups variance to the residual variance. The observed *F*-score can then be converted to a *p*-value, because the distribution of *F*-scores under the null model (i.e., no differences among the group means) is well known (plus, the *F*-**distribution** is built into our PsyStat app). Further, Bayes factors can be computed directly from the observed *F*-score; see Faulkenberry (2018; 2019; 2021) for various methods of doing this computation.

Correlation

Whereas the *t*-test and analysis of variance are used to test for differences among group means, correlation is used to test for a linear *association* between two variables. A **correlation coefficient** is a descriptive statistic (usually denoted r) which ranges from −1 to 1. A correlation coefficient at either of these endpoints denotes a perfect linear association, whereas a correlation coefficient closer to 0 denotes a weaker association. For research questions like "Is there a relationship between X and Y?", a correlation is a good way to answer this. The two models usually considered are a null model where there is no relationship (i.e., the correlation coefficient equals 0), and an alternative model where there IS a relationship. As with the *t*-test and the analysis of variance, the observed data can be transformed into a correlation coefficient, which can then be converted into a *p*-value or Bayes factor.

Linear regression

Correlation is used to test whether there is a relationship between two variables. **Linear regression** takes this one step further by actually estimating the linear equation that relates the two variables. That is, linear regression can be used to estimate the slope and intercept of the linear equation that predicts variable *Y* directly from variable *X*. In fact, linear regression can be extended further to measure how *multiple* variables predict a single outcome variable *Y*.

Computer software resources

Once you've finished with this book, the likelihood that you will do statistics "by hand" is small. Indeed, once you get past the simple *t*-test, doing hand computation gets increasingly tedious. Most likely, you will use computer software packages to do statistics. There are many such packages, but my favorites are the free ones. As of 2021, the "big three" are JASP (https://www.jasp-stats.org), jamovi (https://www.jamovi.org), and R (https://www.r-project.org). Each of these packages enjoys a large user base, and help can be readily obtained via a simple Google search.

Further reading

There are many excellent books on statistics that are focused on its role in psychology and the behavioral sciences. I'll first list and comment on some free ones – these are each available as open source documents and can be freely downloaded, remixed, and shared with others:

- Navarro, D., *Learning Statistics with R.* https://learningstatisticswithr.com

  - I highly recommend this book by Danielle Navarro. Though it is focused on learning statistics via the programming language R, it's clear exposition and detailed coverage of many topics make it a modern classic.

- Navarro, D., & Foxcroft, D., *Learning Statistics with jamovi.* https://learnstatswithjamovi.com

  - This is an adaptation of the previous book that is focused instead on the free statistical software package jamovi.

- Navarro, D., Foxcroft, D., & Faulkenberry, T., *Learning Statistics with JASP.* https://learnstatswithjasp.com

  - Similar to the previous two, this adaptation of Navarro's *Learning Statistics with R* is focused on the free software package JASP.

From here, I will offer a list of seven books that I personally feel are some of the best resources to extend your statistical journey after learning the basics. Please note that for the most part, these are quite advanced, but you these books will have something for everyone.

- Howell, D. C., *Statistical Methods for Psychology* (8th. Edition). Wadsworth: Cengage Learning.

  - This is definitely a traditional textbook for psychological statistics, but I feel it is unmatched among its peers. It covers the traditional topics found in most comprehensive psychological statistics textbooks (except for Bayesian statistics), but it does so at a depth that works for both undergraduate as well as graduate courses. You can go as deep into the topics as you'd like, and there's something for everyone.

- Dienes, Z., *Understanding Psychology as a Science: An Introduction to Scientific and Statistical Inference.* Palgrave McMillan.

  - This is a short book, but it is easily readable and gives a very good overview of statistics and its role in the psychological and behavioral sciences. One of the best parts of this book is that it covers much of the historical basis for statistical inference and traces the development of some of the different methods we covered in this book.

- Box, D. R., *Principles of Statistical Inference.* Cambridge University Press

  - A short book, but definitely a difficult read. Once you've finished Dienes, you can try this one. It is definitely a more mathematically-oriented book, but the rewards for making it through this classic are numerous.

- Cumming, G., & Calin-Jageman, R. *Introduction to the New Statistics: Estimation, Open Science, & Beyond.* Routledge.

  - This book is highly recommended for its alternative approach to inference. Rather than using model comparison as a primary tool for inference, it espouses an approach almost completely based on estimation. If our earlier work with confidence intervals has intrigued you, this will be a great book for you.

- Lambert, B. *A Student's Guide to Bayesian Statistics.* Sage Publications.

  - This is a very good accessible textbook on Bayesian statistics. Like many books on Bayesian statistics, it does have a lot of mathematics contained in it (mostly at the calculus level). But, in spite of this, the explanations given throughout are very thorough and easy to approach.

- Bailer-Jones, C. A. L. *Practical Bayesian Inference: A Primer for Physical Scientists*. Cambridge University Press.

    - Don't let the title fool you; this book is not just for physical scientists. This is another good textbook on Bayesian statistics. There are lots of hands-on examples using the statistical programming language R.

- Lee, M., & Wagenmakers, E.-J. *Bayesian Cognitive Modeling: A Practical Course*. Cambridge University Press.

    - I saved my favorite for last. Written by two well-known mathematical psychologists, *Bayesian Cognitive Modeling* gives the reader a quick exposure to the key aspects of Bayesian statistics through a problem-based learning approach. The book is more like a workbook than a traditional textbook. Instead of just reading, you are invited to work along with the examples and play around with the R code. You'll learn a lot doing this, as I did.

Glossary

alternative hypothesis – see **alternative model**.

alternative model – a statistical model (typically denoted $\mathcal{H}_1$) which states that the population mean is different from some fixed number. Usually used to represent a hypothetical situation where a treatment population mean is different from the mean of the general population. Also called an **alternative hypothesis**.

analysis of variance – a technique for performing statistical inference on a collection of three or more sample means. Instead of testing models of the population mean, the analysis of variance works by partitioning variance of observed data into two sources – the variance between treatments and the variance within treatments – and computes the ratio of these two variances. Inference is performed by comparing this ratio against a standard F-**distribution**.

ANOVA – see **analysis of variance**.

Bayes factor – a number which represents the relative likelihood of some observed data under two different models.

Bayesian model comparison – a method of model comparison that relies on the Bayes factor instead of the p-value to index how well a set of competing models predicts some observed data.

Bayes' Rule – see **Bayes' Theorem**.

Bayes' Theorem – also known as **Bayes' Rule**, it is a mathematical result which formalizes the computation of posterior probability as the prior probability multiplied by an updating factor.

center – in the context of descriptive statistics, a single number that represents a typical measurement in a set of data. Examples include mean and median.

central limit theorem – a mathematical theorem which states that if we have a distribution with mean μ and standard deviation σ, the distribution of sample means that arises from samples of size N is approximately a normal distribution with mean μ and standard deviation $\sigma / \sqrt{N}$. This reduced standard deviation is also called the **standard error of the mean**, or simply, the **standard error**.

confidence interval – an interval of numbers, centered at the mean, within which we have some degree of confidence (usually 95%) that the population mean is contained. Usually used to as a tool for **estimation**.

correlation coefficient – a descriptive statistic that describes the degree of association between two numeric variables. Ranges from −1 to 1.

critical values – in the context of a probability distribution, these are the values that define the outer limits of the interval containing the central 95% of the mass of the distribution. For example, when using the standard normal distribution as a model for the distribution of sample means, the critical values are ±1.96, since 95% of the possible sample means are within 1.96 standard errors from the mean.

degrees of freedom – in the context of a t-test, it is one less than the number of observations. More generally (beyond the scope of this book), it is the number of independent pieces of information which must be known in order to compute a statistical estimate.

descriptive statistics – numerical summaries of a set of measurements. Typically, examples include mean, median, mode, variance, and standard deviation.

deviation score – for a single measurement, the difference between the measurement and the mean.

directional – in the context of research questions, it represents a question of whether a treatment mean changes in a specific direction (i.e., either increases or decreases).

dispersion – a synonym for **variability**.

distribution of sample means – also known as a **sampling distribution**, it is the distribution that arises from repeatedly taking samples of a given size and computing the mean of each sample. By the **central limit theorem**, the distribution of sample means is often modeled by a normal distribution.

effect size – a measure of the impact of an experimental treatment, defined in terms of the observed difference between measurements divided by the standard deviation.

estimation – in the context of statistical inference, it is the process of using confidence intervals to gain information about some unknown population parameter (usually the mean μ).

F-distribution – a model for the ratio of between-treatments variance to within-treatments variance under the null model. Used in the context of an analysis of variance.

frequentist – a theoretical perspective on probability which specifies that probability measures represent the relative long-run frequency of events. For example, a frequentist interpretation of a p-value of 0.05 would consider that the given observed data would only occur 5 times out of 100 if the null model were correct.

Gaussian distribution – see **normal distribution**.

hypothesis testing (also known as model comparison) – the process of assessing which model is most likely to predict some observed data. Hypothesis testing traditionally involves comparing two models against a set of observed data.

independent samples *t*-test – a specific type of *t*-test used for contexts where the goal is to compare the means of two independent, or nonoverlapping, samples.

inflection point – in the context of a probability density function, it is a point where the concavity of the graph changes. For example, in the graph of a normal distribution, the distance from the mean μ to the inflection point is equal to the standard deviation σ.

linear regression – a method of statistical inference where outcome variables can be mathematically predicted from predictor variables.

mean – also known as the average, it is a measure of center that is defined as the sum of the measurements divided by the number of measurements.

median – the middle number of a dataset. It is computed by first arranging the measurements in numerical order and then identifying the measurement in the middle position. If the number of measurements is odd, there will be one unique measurement in the middle – this number is taken as the median. If the number of measurements is even, there will be two measurements in the middle, in which case the median is taken as the average of these two numbers.

mode – in the context of measurements that simply classify membership in a category, the mode is the most frequently occurring measurement.

model – a quantitative instantiation of some observable phenomenon. In this book, models are usually *statistical* models, so they are specified in terms of restricting the values of parameters in some probability distribution.

model comparison (also known as hypothesis testing) – the process of assessing which model is most likely to predict some observed data. Whereas hypothesis testing is traditionally done in the context of two models, model comparison can involve considering any number of candidate models against a set of observed data.

nondirectional – in the context of research questions, it represents a question of whether a treatment mean changes, without any specific prediction of direction for the change.

normal distribution – also known as a **Gaussian distribution**, it is one of the most common probability distributions used in statistical inference. Though it has a specific mathematical definition, it is usually described as mound-shaped and symmetric about its center. It is completely described by two parameters: the mean μ and the standard deviation σ.

null hypothesis – see **null model**.

null hypothesis testing – a classical form of model comparison which is based on computing the probability of observing some specific data if the null hypothesis is true.

null model – a statistical model (typically denoted $\mathcal{H}_0$) which states that the population mean is equal to some fixed number. Usually used to represent a hypothetical situation where a treatment population mean is no different from the mean of the general population. Also called a **null hypothesis.**

one-tailed test – a model comparison or hypothesis test in which the alternative model is directional. It is called "one-tailed" because the p-value comes from only one tail of the comparison distribution.

parameter – a number which specifies some essential component of a probability distribution. They are typically denoted by a Greek letter. For example, in the normal distribution, the center of the distribution is specified by the parameter μ and the variability of the distribution is specified by the parameter σ.

paired-samples t-test – a specific type of t-test used in repeated measures designs. Instead of computing the mean score among a single set of measurements, the observed scores are calculated as the difference between the two repeated measurements for each experimental unit.

percentile rank – for a specific measurement in a larger set of measurements, it is the proportion of measurements with numeric value less than that specific measurement.

population – in the context of a research question, this is the set of all observable units (e.g., people) to which I want to generalize an observable phenomenon.

posterior probability – in the context of Bayesian inference, it is the probability of a specific model after observing data.

prior probability – in the context of Bayesian inference, it is the probability of a specific model prior to observing data.

probability density function – see **probability distribution.**

probability distribution – a mathematical function (also called a **probability density function**) which formally expresses the likelihood of all possible measurements/outcomes.

p-value – a number that expresses the probability of obtaining an actually observed sample mean (or more extreme) if the null model is correct. Indexes the plausibility of observed data under the null.

sample – a subset of a population that is actually observed/measured.

sampling distribution – see **distribution of sample means.**

spread – a synonym for **variability.**

standard deviation – a measure of variability, defined as the square root of variance. Compared to variance, standard deviation has the advantage of being on the same scale as the original measurements.

standard error – see **standard error of the mean.**

standard error of the mean – computed as $\sigma / \sqrt{N}$, it is the standard deviation of the distribution of sample means for samples of size N.

standard normal distribution – a normal distribution with $\mu = 0$ and $\sigma = 1$.

statistical inference – the process of using parameter estimation and model comparison to justify population-level claims about observable phenomena using observed sample data.

statistically significant – a descriptive phrase which implies that an observed relationship would be very rare if there was indeed no relationship at the population level.

Student's *t*-distribution – see *t*-distribution.

t-distribution – also known as **Student's *t*-distribution**, it is a model for the distribution of sample means that is obtained whenever the population standard deviation σ is estimated from observed data. In simple cases, the *t*-distribution has one parameter the **degrees of freedom** – and this parameter controls the shape of the distribution.

t-test – a model comparison procedure used when the population standard deviation σ is unknown. In this case, σ is estimated from data, and the resulting distribution of sample means follows a *t*-distribution rather than a normal distribution.

two-tailed test – a model comparison or hypothesis test in which the alternative model is nondirectional. It is called "two-tailed" because the *p*-value comes from both tails of the comparison distribution.

variability – in the context of descriptive statistics, a single number which represents the extent to which the measurements in a set of data differ from the most typical measurement. Examples include standard deviation and variance.

variance – a measure of variability, defined as the average squared deviation from the mean. Compared to standard deviation, the variance is not as commonly used as a descriptive measure of variability because the scale is squared compared to the original measurement units.

z-score – a common method of standardizing measurements, defined as the distance from a measurement to the mean, divided by the standard deviation.

Answers to end-of-chapter exercises

Chapter 2

1 mean = 8, median = 7, variance = 17.6, standard deviation = 4.20
2 mean increases by 2, but standard deviation does not change.
3 $z = 1.25$, $z = -0.50$, $z = 2.00$
4 43.75, 53.75

Chapter 3

1 a. 0.309; b. 0.788; c. 0.683
2 a. 0.00383; b. 0.0874; c. 0.473
3 0.467
4 a. 0.337; b. 0.0973

Chapter 4

1 a. 0.159; b. 0.0228; c. 0.261
2 a. 0.309; b. 0.202; c. 0.451
3 a. 0.703; b. 0.825
4 a. 0.0765; b. 0.00398; c. 0.0693

Chapter 5

1 a. (18.80, 31.20); b. (20.62, 29.38); c. the interval gets narrower.
2 a. (29.08, 36.92); b. 0.0668; c. No, data are plausible under the null.
3 a. (41.04, 44.96); b. 0.00135; c. Yes, the data are rare under the null.
4 Yes. For the sample, we have $z = 2.63$, $p = 0.00427$, so reject null.

Chapter 6

1 Yes. For the sample, we have $t = 2.18$, $p = 0.0228$, so reject null.
2 a. No; for the sample, we have $t = 1.13$, $p = 0.135$, so fail to reject null.
   b. Yes; for the sample, we have $t = 1.80$, $p = 0.0383$, so reject null. c. As

sample size increases, the likelihood of rejecting null (for same observed data) increases.

3 Yes. For the sample, we have $t = 2.69$, $p = 0.0168$, so reject null.

4 (13.73, 15.27).

Chapter 7

1 No. $t = 0.40$, $BF_{01} = 5.12$, posterior probability of null = 0.8366.

2 Yes. $t = -3.83$, $BF_{10} = 83.63$, posterior probability of alternative = 0.9882.

3 No. $t = 1.31$, $BF_{01} = 1.60$, posterior probability of null = 0.6153.

4 Yes, $t = 2.69$, $BF_{10} = 3.58$, posterior probability of alternative = 0.7816.

References

Atkinson, R. C., & Shiffrin, R. M. (1968). Human memory: A proposed system and its control processes. In Spence, K. W., & Spence, J. T. (eds.) *The psychology of learning and motivation (volume 2)*. New York, NY: Academic Press. pp. 89–195.

Busemeyer, J. R., & Diederich, A. (2010). *Cognitive modeling*. Thousand Oaks, CA: Sage Publications.

Croft, M., & Beard, J. J. (2021). Development and evolution of the SAT and ACT. In Clauser, B. E., & Bunch, M. B. (eds.) *The history of educational measurement: Key advancements in theory, policy, and practice*. New York, NY: Routledge. pp. 1–20.

Cumming, G. (2012). *Understanding the new statistics: Effect sizes, confidence intervals, and meta-analysis*. New York, NY: Routledge.

Cumming, G., & Calin-Jageman, R. (2017). *Introduction to the new statistics: Estimation, open science, & beyond*. New York, NY: Routledge.

Farrell, S., & Lewandowsky, S. (2018). *Computational modeling of cognition and behavior*. Cambridge, UK: Cambridge University Press.

Faulkenberry, T. J. (2018). Computing Bayes factors to measure evidence from experiments: An extension of the BIC approximation. *Biometrical Letters*, 55 (1), 31–43. https://doi.org/10.2478/bile-2018-0003

Faulkenberry, T. J. (2019). Estimating evidential value from analysis of variance summaries: A comment on Ly et al. (2018). *Advances in Methods and Practices in Psychological Science*, 2 (4), 406–409. https://doi.org/10.1177/2515245919872960

Faulkenberry, T. J. (2021). The Pearson Bayes factor: An analytic formula for computing evidential value from minimal summary statistics. *Biometrical Letters*, 58 (1), 1–26. https://doi.org/10.2478/bile-2021-0001

Faulkenberry, T. J., Ly, A., & Wagenmakers, E.-J. (2020). Bayesian inference in numerical cognition: A tutorial using JASP. *Journal of Numerical Cognition*, 6 (2), 231–259. https://doi.org/10.5964/jnc.v6i2.288

Gigerenzer, G. (2004). Mindless statistics. *The Journal of Socio-Economics*, 33 (5), 587–606. https://doi.org/10.1016/j.socec.2004.09.033

Goldberg, L. R. (1993). The structure of phenotypic personality traits. *American Psychologist*, 48 (1). 26–34. https://doi.org/10.1037/0003-066X.48.1.26

Henik, A., & Tzelgov, J. (1982). Is three greater than five: The relation between physical and semantic size in comparison tasks. *Memory & Cognition*, 10 (4), 389–395. https://doi.org/10.3758/bf03202431

Hoekstra, R., Morey, R. D., Rouder, J. N., & Wagenmakers, E.-J. (2014). Robust misinterpretation of confidence intervals. *Psychonomic Bulletin & Review*, 21 (5), 1157–1164. https://doi.org/10.3758/s13423-013-0572-3

Hoel, P. G. (1984). *Introduction to mathematical statistics* (5th ed.). New York, NY: Wiley.

JASP Team. (2020). JASP (Version 0.14.1). https://jasp-stats.org

Jeffreys H. (1961). *Theory of probability.* Oxford, UK: Oxford University Press.

Kanizsa, G. (1976). Subjective contours. *Scientific American, 234* (4), 48–52. https://doi.org/10.1038/scientificamerican0476-48

Kass, R., & Raftery, A. (1995). Bayes factors. *Journal of the American Statistical Association, 90* (430), 773–795. https://doi.org/10.2307/2291091

Larson, H. J. (1995). *Introduction to probability.* Reading, MA: Addison-Wesley.

Ly, A., Raj, A., Etz, A., Marsman, M., Gronau, Q. F., & Wagenmakers, E.-J. (2018). Bayesian reanalyses from summary statistics: A guide for academic consumers. *Advances in Methods and Practices in Psychological Science, 1*, 367–374. https://doi.org/10.1177/2515245918779348

Lee, M. D., & Wagenmakers, E.-J. (2013). *Bayesian cognitive modeling: A practical course.* Cambridge, UK: Cambridge University Press.

McGrayne, S. B. (2012). *The theory that would not die: How Bayes' rule cracked the Enigma Code, hunted down Russian submarines, & emerged triumphant from two centuries of controversy.* New Haven, CT: Yale University Press.

Miller, J. (1988). A warning about median reaction time. *Journal of Experimental Psychology: Human Perception and Performance, 14* (3), 539–543. https://doi.org/10.1037/0096-1523.14.3.539

Morey, R. D., Rouder, J. N., Verhagen, J., & Wagenmakers, E.-J. (2014). Why hypothesis tests are essential for psychological science. *Psychological Science, 25* (6), 1289–1290. https://doi.org/10.1177/0956797614525969

Navarro, D., Foxcroft, D., & Faulkenberry, T. J. (2019). *Learning statistics with JASP: A tutorial for psychology students and other beginners.* https://www.learnstatswithjasp.com

Pruim, R. (2018). *Foundations and applications of statistics: An introduction using R* (2nd ed.). Providence, RI: American Mathematical Society.

Rouder, J. N., Speckman, P. L., Sun, D., Morey, R. D., & Iverson, G. (2009). Bayesian t tests for accepting and rejecting the null hypothesis. *Psychonomic Bulletin & Review, 16* (2), 225–237. https://doi.org/10.3758/pbr.16.2.225

Rouder, J. N., Engelhardt, C. R., McCabe, S., & Morey, R. D. (2016). Model comparison in ANOVA. *Psychonomic Bulletin & Review, 23* (6), 1779–1786. https://doi.org/10.3758/s13423-016-1026-5

Sherman, E. (2020, August 31). College tuition is rising at twice the inflation rate – while students learn at home. https://www.forbes.com/sites/zengernews/2020/08/31/college-tuition-is-rising-at-twice-the-inflation-rate-while-students-learn-at-home/

Twenge, J. M. (2000). The age of anxiety? The birth cohort change in anxiety and neuroticism, 1952–1993. *Journal of Personality and Social Psychology, 79* (6), 1007–1021. https://doi.org/10.1037/0022-3514.79.6.1007

Wagenmakers, E.-J., Lee, M. D., Rouder, J. N., & Morey, R. D. (2020). The principle of predictive irrelevance or why intervals should not be used for model comparison featuring a point null hypothesis. In Gruber, C. W. (ed.) *The theory of statistics in psychology* (111–129). Switzerland: Springer Nature AG. https://doi.org/10.1007/978-3-030-48043-1_8

Wagenmakers, E.-J., Wetzels, R., Borsboom, D., & van der Maas, H. L. J. (2011). *Why psychologists must change the way they analyze their data: The case of psi: Comment on Bem (2011). Journal of Personality and Social Psychology, 100*, 426–432. https://doi.org/10.1037/a0022790

Wechsler, D. (2008). Wechsler Adult Intelligence Scale–Fourth Edition (WAIS-IV) [Database record]. *APA PsycTests.* https://doi.org/10.1037/t15169-000

Wilcox, R. (2010). *Fundamentals of modern statistical methods* (2nd ed.). New York, NY: Springer.

Wilcox, R. R. (2017). *Introduction to robust estimation and hypothesis testing* (4th ed.). Boston, MA: Academic Press.

Index

Printed in the United States
by Baker & Taylor Publisher Services